THE POSSIBILITY OF DIFFERENCE

A BIBLICAL AFFIRMATION OF INCLUSIVITY

MARCUS GREEN

kevin mayhew

kevin
mayhew

First published in Great Britain in 2018
by Kevin Mayhew Ltd, Buxhall, Stowmarket, Suffolk IP14 3BW
Tel: +44 (0) 1449 737978 Fax: +44 (0) 1449 737834
E-mail: info@kevinmayhew.com

www.kevinmayhew.com

9 8 7 6 5 4 3 2 1 0

ISBN 978 1 84867 972 6
Catalogue No. 1501595

Cover design by Rob Mortonson
© Images used under licence from Shutterstock Inc.
Edited by Virginia Rounding
Typeset by Angela Selfe
Printed and bound in Great Britain

ABOUT THE AUTHOR

Marcus Green is an Anglican clergyman working in North Oxfordshire. His first book, *Salvation's Song*, published by Survivor Books, was an exploration of the importance of worship in St Matthew's Gospel. It demonstrated how we can see worship most clearly at the cross, and how sight of that worship transforms us completely. He also contributed to *Journeys in Grace and Truth*, published as a resource for the General Synod of the Church of England when it considered matters of human sexuality in the summer of 2016.

Marcus shares his rectory with a springer spaniel, and enjoys a range of activities from skiing and singing with his own jazz quartet to watching football and opera.

COMMENDATIONS OF *THE POSSIBILITY OF DIFFERENCE*

This is a measured, compassionate plea for a more humane argument about sexuality in the Church – a model of debate which avoids polarising language and insistent emotion while drawing on deep personal and spiritual resources.

Archbishop Rowan Williams

I love the way Marcus Green has written this book. His conversational style is honest, attractive and easy to read. But don't let that delude you into thinking he isn't making a serious argument concerning Scripture, culture and mission. The great gift of this book is that it makes familiar (and less familiar) arguments on sexuality eminently accessible. An evangelical writing with a warm heart, full of love both for Scripture and for his fellow Christians, this is a thoughtful, non-confrontational and significant book.

Bishop John Pritchard, former Bishop of Oxford

I've known Marcus since he was a curate at St Michael's Aberystwyth, leading worship and heading up youth work. He later transformed a parish in Pontypridd in the South Wales valleys, establishing an evangelical ministry which continues to flourish, as well as being part of the leadership team for New Wine Wales. Through all those years his passion for Jesus and his commitment to clear Bible teaching shone through. They shine through this book too – which is a gift to anyone who wants to take a fresh look at the thorny questions of human sexuality and the Church today. Marcus clearly loves the Scriptures, wrestles with hard texts and in them finds a God who loves people – all people, whether straight or gay. I'm delighted he has written this timely book.

Bishop Andy John, Bishop of Bangor

Nothing is more needed in our current ecclesial debates about sexual ethics than a pastorally sensitive, exegetically sound, and theologically insightful work which takes the human element as serious as the divine. Marcus Green is not only a great thinker, a thorough academic, and a great pastor, but he is also a fantastic human being. With a humanising touch, Green addresses a subject which too often falls into dehumanising rhetoric or abstracted discussions of ethics. The Church is starving for this book. The world is starving for the Church to say what this book says.

Tom Fuerst, Author, Theologian and Church Planter

I am happy to commend Marcus Green's excellent book. In it he succeeds in setting out his views on gay identity, lifestyle, marriage and ministry in a way that is at once biblical, sensible, disarmingly easy reading and without rancour or stridency. It is the heartfelt witness of a fine evangelical minister to what his prayer life and study have led him to understand, and deserves to be both read and heeded by the contemporary Church.

Peter Southwell, Theologian, University of Oxford, and former Senior Tutor at Wycliffe Hall, Oxford

I have thoroughly enjoyed reading *The Possibility of Difference* – notwithstanding the pain that lies behind so much of what Marcus Green is writing about. I think that it provides a very useful contribution to the current debates . . . My own feeling was that the Romans section was the best, as it highlighted the theme of the validity of a difference of exegesis, as an evangelical, very clearly.
Bishop Colin Fletcher, Bishop of Dorchester

This a most compelling plea to those engaging in both sides of the debate on same sex issues, to listen carefully, honestly, and without judgementalism to the experience of those with whom they disagree. Marcus Green tackles some of the biblical questions and gives a moving account of his own experience. Although not agreeing with his conclusions myself, his longing for 'loving disagreement' is a valuable balance to the tendency of some LGBT campaigners to label every disagreement as homophobia, and of some evangelicals to 'write off' their opponents from their fellowship.
Canon David MacInnes, former Rector of St Aldate's Oxford

At last! This is the book that so many within the Christian Church have been waiting for! A thoroughly engaging, thoroughly researched, profound and moving exposition of the Scriptures in relation to human sexuality and the gospel. In his warm and personable style, Marcus courageously models the very 'loving disagreement' he longs for. I pray that this will mark a whole new chapter in the Church's discussions on sexuality, and provide a much-needed resource that will draw people into respectful dialogue with each other.
Jayne Ozanne, Writer, Director of the Ozanne Foundation

This is a visionary and prophetic book, a timely contribution to the current conversations in the Church . . . In an engaging and captivating style, Marcus lays out a 're-envisioned' understanding of Scripture, carefully exploring the key texts and offering possible new ways of reading them in context, unhindered by cultural baggage and sometimes sloppy translation. Addressing overarching themes of idolatry and true worship, being equally human rather than 'utterly unredeemable' with a positive theological rigour, Marcus invites his readers to explore a 'deeper grace'. His love for Jesus, and for the Church, shines through as he explores the possibility of differing 'with open Bibles, open hearts, honest faith and genuine desire to be true to Jesus and godly in how we live our lives'. I wholeheartedly commend this book and hope it will be widely read by people of all traditions as we continue to learn more about disagreeing well.

Nikki Groarke, Archdeacon of Dudley and member of General Synod

The Possibility of Difference by Marcus Green is a timely and very helpful resource for the Church in the midst of the ongoing difficult debate about human sexuality. Combining his long experience of pastoral parish ministry with evident theological expertise, Marcus helpfully and sensitively explores Scripture, the human condition and pastoral realities in a way that clearly displays his underlying commitment to seeing the flourishing of individuals and of the Church. This book gives a passionate call for unity within the Church, but a unity based on respect and honest engagement with Scripture and difference, and not a false or shallow unity dependent on glossing over and minimising the very real questions that confront us and that both our society and our personal integrity require us to acknowledge and face up to. This book is a rich and warm resource, offering light where far too often we have only had heat. I commend it, not only as a source of valuable teaching, but also – far more importantly – as an aid and a spur to honest, respectful and constructive dialogue.

The Venerable Gavin Collins, Archdeacon of the Meon and member of General Synod

COMMENDATIONS OF PREVIOUS PUBLICATIONS:

Salvation's Song:

This book helps us to 'worship with understanding' – an essential thing for the singing church today.
Matt Redman

Salvation's Song is a great book . . . I've been hugely inspired and convicted as I've delved into this book. I'd encourage all to read it.
Tim Hughes

What a wonderful stimulus to think seriously and creatively about worship! Marcus Green has done us all a service with this wonderful book.
Alister McGrath

This is a liberating and exciting book, which has the potential to open up some very new channels in mission. Marcus Green writes out of a tough and varied pastoral experience, with consummate skills in exegesis as well as a fine ear for the particular human stories woven into his theology.
Archbishop Rowan Williams

'An Ordinary Bloke' (chapter within Journeys in Grace and Truth):

Fascinating, moving and . . . highly engaging.
Ian Paul

CONTENTS

FOREWORD

I know, I know . . . we've already had loads of books on Christian responses to homosexuality. We've needed them (perhaps) because the Church at this particular time is caught up in internal squabbles on the subject and is facing society's incomprehension and irritation.

So why another book?

Because this one has the unique gift of being personal, courteous and eminently approachable. Marcus Green writes as a convinced evangelical who lives with his homosexuality in a relaxed and thoughtful way, loving his Lord and wanting to live in a Big House where there exists the 'possibility of difference'.

I met Marcus in the underbelly of Blackwell's bookshop in Oxford some time ago and congratulated him on his generous submission to a Church of England report on gay relationships. I asked if he had thought of writing it up in more substantial form. And now he has.

Evangelicals who write from his particular standpoint know that they put themselves in the firing line, under suspicion from conservative evangelicals, and their writing seen as unnecessary by those who think the arguments over Scripture are done and dusted. I well remember my colleague on the staff of Cranmer Hall, Durham, Michael Vasey – himself both gay and firmly evangelical – writing an early salvo in this debate called *Strangers and Friends*. As a result, some friends became strangers and some strangers became confused friends, but it was an uncomfortable place for Michael to be, and many were caught in the crossfire.

I am all the more grateful, therefore, that Marcus has been prepared to write of his own thinking, and to do so in such a readable style. Make no mistake, he is passionate about the gospel and about the centrality of Scripture, but he has a wide-angle view of Scripture on this subject and wants to urge his fellow evangelicals to consider it. And 'consider it' is very much the tone of the book. There's no hectoring, no overt defensiveness nor crusading zeal. Indeed, the tone is delightfully honest, and almost innocent, in desiring deeply that Christians of all stripes, and evangelicals in particular, should faithfully look at the evidence again, and embrace the possibility of difference, so we can all move on in mission.

I share that desire. I love the sentiment in Faber's hymn 'There's a wideness in God's mercy, like the wideness of the sea; there's a kindness in his justice, which is more than liberty . . . For the love of God is broader than the scope of human mind, and the heart of the Eternal is most wonderfully kind.' I don't think that's sentimentality; I think that's honest theology. God is always more. Divine abundance will always flood the narrow pathways of human understanding.

My hope is that this book, with its winning style, will appeal to many who have grown weary with much reading in this area, and that its biblical, theological, personal and missional matrix will open up fresh channels of grace for the Spirit to use.

Thank you, Marcus. Dear reader, over to you.

John Pritchard

INTRODUCTION

I have a confession to make: I'm an Anglican. That's a complicated thing to say these days. Truth is, it's always been that way.

One of the key understandings of Anglicanism is that it is a 'big house': if my Father's home has many mansions, then this wing of his home delights in all the variety that might entail. I am an evangelical within that 'big house' because I have always believed it is the best way of understanding and following Jesus (I guess that counts as another confession). Yet I also see that within my Church there exist others whose path of faith is different to mine, equally heartfelt, at times challenging, but also very genuine. As an evangelical, I don't do humility terribly well. (No need; I'm right most of the time . . .) But there are those moments when, in the 'big house', if I'm honest, I have to admit I find my fellow residents grasping something 'other' of Jesus that I know I miss. Sometimes they grasp it so clearly that (despite myself) I want to understand more of where they are coming from. It pains me to say it, but truth must out.

As an evangelical, I know that the Church of England was founded on good reformed protestant, evangelical doctrine. As a former history student, I have to add the C of E also always had room for catholic practice. That was the deal: Catholic and Reformed. The balance between these (sometimes uneasy room-mates) has shifted through the years. And, of course, as theological liberalism developed, that too became an intrinsic part of the deal. A church that sees itself as 'a church for everyone' can at times be an uncomfortable place.

Well, comfort isn't everything.

These days evangelicalism itself is a 'big house'. Times change: at the end of the nineteenth century, the Anglo-Catholic wing of the Church of England was in the ascendant; through the mid and latter parts of the twentieth century, the liberal side of the Church was so prevalent that at times many evangelicals felt as though they were fighting for their right to exist. Yet as the twenty-first century settles in, the archbishoprics of Canterbury and York are both held in evangelical hands, large evangelical churches are growing in all sorts of unexpected places, and we have so much space and so many members that we take leisure time to disagree with each other within our own camp on virtually everything that comes our way.

Virtually everything?

We disagree on ethics: for example, evangelicals take strongly differing views on divorce and the remarriage of divorcees in church. A few will still take a very strict, traditional reading of the Scriptures, arguing against allowing any divorce at all and certainly not countenancing remarriage – especially not in church. This used to be the standard line. I dare say that most of us who have been ordained more than five minutes remember those days. It's a minority stance now. Perhaps it's true that more might like to stay with this position, but feel the pastoral pull of the people in their care and therefore end up holding a theoretically strict stance whilst actually conducting services of blessing for second marriages. Some evangelicals view marriage as an ordinance of God and a simple 'good' that should always be there for all men and women – forgiveness reigns, lines are drawn over the past, a new day brings a new life, and all are welcome here. We differ; but we are all evangelical. We know this is not the heart of the gospel. We get on with each other, if not always entirely approving of our neighbours.

We disagree on church order: even within the confines of Anglican evangelicalism, there is a wide variety of theologies and practices when it comes to (for example) baptism. All lay claim to some biblical precedent: believer's baptism or infant baptism – is the emphasis on our response to God's love or on his offer of love to us in the first place? How much water would you like with your baptism? A sprinkle or a dunking, or something in between? Even the chap in my local camera shop has an opinion on this: just recently, as I went to buy some developing fluid, I was given a lecture on the correct understanding of the Bible and baptism! Virtually every evangelical parish in the land seems to have developed its own slightly different order of service and style of preparation (God bless cut-and-paste liturgy); and virtually every evangelical minister is happy for his fellows to do so. We differ, but we are all evangelical. We know that, whilst this is important, it is not quite the heart of the gospel. So we get on with each other, if sometimes smiling knowingly about the folk down the road.

We even (hush, don't say it out loud!) disagree on doctrine: to listen to some of us evangelicals, you'd think the Holy Spirit was the first person of the Trinity; to listen to others, you'd be forgiven for thinking you were back in Ephesus in Acts 19 with those disciples who hadn't even heard there was a Holy Spirit. Charismatic gifts – are they essential signs of godliness or a satanic deception? Take your pick. Most British evangelicals

(Anglicans to the fore, but Methodists, Baptists and all joining the Spring Harvest/New Wine parade) seem to have basically gone for the former option over the last twenty years, where even traditional village churches can be found to have healing prayer groups and services. And, of course, there are very strong congregations that still hold to something pretty close to the latter opinion.

Now this is no minor issue. The Holy Spirit is God; we are talking about who God is and how he deals with us. This is crucial theology, surely a first order matter (if we can ever agree any pecking order of what is truly important), and certainly a large part of New Testament writing. Yet we evangelicals differ. We agree that this is very important, but we somehow allow that we are united on Jesus who is at the heart of the gospel and upon his death upon the Cross for us and his Resurrection – though how we so thoroughly separate Jesus and the Spirit remains a brilliant theological sleight of hand. Remarkably, in a forced kind of way, at a distance preferably, we even manage to get on – though having the occasional common 'enemy' to focus on helps us deal with each other when we have to.

Evangelicals therefore differ on ethics, church order and doctrine and still manage to be evangelicals. Truly we are ourselves a 'big house'. Generous old-fashioned Anglican principles of Christian latitude are working well – evangelicals are almost the modern version of the old Jewish joke – put two evangelicals in a room, get three opinions.[1]

---

1. Clearly, this is a simplification of the question of adiaphora. Bishop N. T. Wright's Presidential Address to the Durham Synod in May 2010 is more thorough and nuanced, even if I wouldn't agree with all his conclusions: http://ntwrightpage.com/2016/04/05/diocese-of-durham-diocesan-synod-may-21-2010/. The 2016 Primates Conference final communique –www.anglicancommunion.org/media/206035/Communiqué_from_the_Primates_Meeting_2016.pdf – is a case study of how to live in the 'big house'.

Well, until we get to the real contemporary test of orthodoxy, in which case suddenly we find there is almost no room for us to differ with each other at all.

The real contemporary test of orthodoxy? It's a bit bizarre, because it's not in any of the historic creeds. It's not in any early church statement of faith, and it is absent from the Reformers' great debates. Luther didn't make any great play on this. Calvin didn't seem to care. The Westminster Shorter Catechism forgot to focus here.

But now – well, now we know better.

Now the real contemporary test of genuine and true Christian orthodoxy is: what is our attitude to homosexuality? The claim is that, historically, all evangelicalism has been monolithic in its response to this single issue. It's an ethics question – and behaviourally, all homosexual acts must be seen as wrong. Period. It's a church order question – and practising homosexuals should never be in leadership, never be clergy, and no homosexuals should ever think of being bishops. It's a theological question – because we are told clearly that it goes to the very heart of how we handle the Scriptures, and to question these positions is to doubt the authority of the Scriptures themselves and therefore to place our own authority higher than God's.

Of course, in quiet, over a cup of coffee and with no one really listening, and with the passing of time and the advancement of younger leaders, this caricature isn't the entire truth. Notable evangelicals have put their heads above the parapet: in Britain, Bishop James Jones in Liverpool was perhaps the highest profile evangelical in the English Anglican scene first to do so.[2] Steve Chalke has written of the need to reassess the debate[3] (and been much criticised for it[4]). The position of these few voices often seems to be pastoral (people are people and need caring for – words which are hard to gainsay) or cultural (the world has changed, let's face reality – another truism) rather than more solidly based on actual biblical interpretation, which surely ought to be the reason for evangelicals altering their standpoint.

When biblical interpretation gets mentioned, conservative evangelical commentators have sometimes seemed to respond either by condemning methodology or resorting to personal attacks (you don't know how to look at the Scriptures properly/ you're not really an evangelical) rather than by engaging more fully with content, and Steve Chalke is amongst those who have taken some hits on this;[5] the same happened to Jayne Ozanne's collection of essays for General Synod in 2016.[6]

The change in our culture and the power of this debate have perhaps most clearly been seen as some notable, and very different, evangelicals have publicly identified themselves as gay in recent years. The way this has happened has demonstrated some of the power of this test of orthodoxy.

Vaughan Roberts, author, rector of St Ebbe's in Oxford and president of the conservative evangelical Proclamation Trust, explained in an interview in the magazine *Evangelicals Now* in

---

2. See http://www.telegraph.co.uk/news/religion/9934686/Senior-Church-of-England-bishop-calls-for-gay-union-blessing-services.html

3. See http://www.christianitymagazine.co.uk/sexuality/stevechalke.aspx

4. See https://www.fulcrum-anglican.org.uk/articles/scriptural-faithfulness-inclusion-and-truth-in-pastoral-care-a-response-to-steve-chalke/ which will serve as an example.

5. Fulcrum, ibid.

6. Jayne Ozanne (ed.), *Journeys in Game and Truth*, Ekklesia, 2016. An example of the response to this, questioning the participants in the book, comes from Ian Paul's typically robust blog post in July 2016: https://www.psephizo.com/sexuality-2/journeying-in-grace-and-truth/

2012 that he was writing out of his own experience when he wrote about Christian attitudes to homosexuality.[7] Vaughan is a thoughtful, intelligent man whose writing and self-expression are always carefully nuanced. He is theologically very conservative and holds to traditional teachings on sexuality. It wasn't a matter of 'coming out' for him, as this might suggest embracing a gay identity. Vaughan sees that as rejecting God's best plans. Vaughan's interview was a matter of 'being more open' in a world where the alternative can be fear and shame, qualities which can be destructive in any life.

Vaughan lives an exemplary life, is an exemplary teacher and puts forward powerful, personal arguments for holding to traditional, conservative theologies and practices regarding understandings of homosexuality. Being gay is not a phrase he embraces; he talks of same-sex attraction, and for him this means being single and celibate. As difficult as it must have been to speak, Vaughan remains very highly respected within evangelicalism. I might add that, in my experience, those who follow him don't always get the nuances that Vaughan appreciates; and I don't think it's unfair to say that, in his writings, he scores very high on the contemporary orthodoxy test.

In August 2014 the *Independent* newspaper published an article featuring songwriter, worship-leader, theologian and media presenter Vicky Beeching.[8] She wasn't just 'more open'; she came out as gay.

Vicky's words were very personal, they drew heavily upon her life story, and told of loneliness and even spiritual abuse. The article was picked up by other newspapers and ran as TV news.

---

7. Vaughan Roberts, 'A Battle I Face', *Evangelicals Now*, October 2012.
8. Vicky Beeching, 'Christian Rock Star: I'm gay, God loves me just the way I am', *Independent*, 13 August 2014.

Repeatedly, throughout the subsequent radio and TV exposure, Vicky spoke confidently, calmly and powerfully of the inhumanity of fearing to reveal her sexuality. Her media contacts gave her enormous public support. She seemed to have no interest in what score she might get on the contemporary orthodoxy test. But some churches stopped using her songs; she drew sharply critical responses on social media as well as finding great support; and her previous public Christian life had changed beyond recognition.

In the States, the stakes have in many respects been even higher, and yet some evangelicals are beginning to try to change the narrative. Justin Lee established the Gay Christian Network as a strong voice drawing together gay Christians who disagree on all sorts of things but who wish to remain faithful to Jesus and to their evangelical roots. His book *Unconditional*[9] (*Torn* in the US) focuses heavily on his personal experience rather than on the theology of the debate, and is either a red rag to a bull or a sign of hope in a sea of despair – depending where you sit.

Demonstrating the size of the 'Big House', Ed Shaw offers his book *The Plausibility Problem*,[10] drawing on his own struggles to encourage young folk experiencing what he refers to as 'same-sex attraction' to stick to a more traditional way of understanding. He cares about that orthodoxy test, and about keeping other people the right side of it.

Hmm.

---

9. Justin Lee, *Unconditional: Rescuing the Gospel from the Gays-vs-Christians Debate*, Hodder, 2013.
10. Ed Shaw, *The Plausibility Problem: the Church and Same-Sex Attraction*, InterVarsity Press, 2015.

Well, I have a question about this contemporary test of orthodoxy.

Experience is one thing; we all have stories to tell. However, having demonstrated that evangelicals are a varied bunch with varied tastes and outlooks on life and God whilst still holding firm to the same Scriptures with the same fervour and outlook and understanding and heart and soul, my starter question is not so much about experience and story (though I may come back to this shortly). What I want to know is: might it be possible for an evangelical to hold a different view on sexuality to the usual party line, but a different view which actually has its basis in the Scriptures? A view that belongs fully to the way in which we evangelicals handle the Scriptures? Genuinely? Might there be here too, on this most contentious of current issues, the possibility of difference between us within our own ranks – a difference that allows for thoughtfulness and consideration without the wholesale dismantling of treasured belief systems? Might it be possible to voice a different opinion and yet be an evangelical on the basis not just of care for others or desire to be true to those around us or on our own valid experience but also on the basis of seeking a better understanding of familiar texts and the whole counsel of Scripture?

I'm grateful for the work of folk like Matthew Vines and his *God and the Gay Christian*.[11] He takes the story of experience and adds a much deeper level of biblical understanding as he asks questions of traditional interpretations of texts that have always been understood to show why Christians shouldn't

---

11. Matthew Vines, *God and the Gay Christian: The Biblical Case in Support of Same-Sex Relationships*, Convergent, 2014.

accept a gay agenda. But I want to push past these texts. I want to go deeper.

I want to ask, not can we question, but can we smash this orthodoxy test?

My question is not hiding a secret agenda that everyone should suddenly throw away their Bibles and believe something different. In what follows – and please hear this – I have no need at all for everyone to change their thinking and in one sudden moment of realisation start seeing the world as I do. And I certainly don't want anyone to throw their Bible away. That would be (frankly) ridiculous, and against everything I hold dear as an evangelical. But I can't help wondering if it might be perfectly fair for true and thorough-going evangelicals to break the taboo on homosexuality not because we have succumbed to the spirit of the age, but because we are all humbly trying to submit to the whole word of God? That's my kind of *adiaphora* – where we evangelicals (along with everyone else) address issues beyond the nature of God and redemption as honest Christians with open Bibles, openly pushing each other to a better understanding through debate and difference.

It's good to talk. It's vital to challenge places where talking feels forbidden.

So I will tackle some of the Scriptures usually taken to enforce the common evangelical party attitude to homosexuality and ask some serious questions of them. But that's just the beginning. Having asked those questions, let's see where we are, and where the Scriptures say we need to go.

And yes, I'm asking for the possibility of difference here because it affects me personally. Hands up, guilty. (Back to story and experience.) If my first confession was that I'm an Anglican and my second was that I'm an evangelical, my third is that I'm gay. It's fair to say that my experience makes me want to work on my theology.

Bringing these things together has its moments.

In the early 2000s, I appeared on the BBC TV quiz show 'The Weakest Link'. You might remember the programme. In the UK it used to be on every day of the week, just before the six o'clock news. Anne Robinson set up contestant after contestant with her acerbic wit, only to knock them down and make poor members of the public look like fools as they tried to appear clever on the way to winning not very much cash.

I was on this show.

And, being in my mid-thirties, a vicar, and single, it suddenly occurred to me in the days before filming that Anne would ask if I was gay. It's a stereotype that she rarely avoided. I am gay, but also evangelical, and back fifteen years ago when this happened I had hardly ever told anyone. I lived with the daily internal struggle that this produced. It wasn't easy. It was often very lonely. Even my parents didn't know. I wanted to be able to work as an evangelical in the Church, and I wasn't about to come out on national TV.

But nor was I about to lie if asked a direct question.

So, I spent a day – an entire day – thinking through what my answer would be, should Anne ask me at any time if I was gay.

When she did so, on camera, in the middle of the quiz ('Marcus: you're 36, a vicar and single: are you gay?') my 'off the cuff' reply was a relaxed, smiling, deflecting, 'Are you checking to see if I'm available, Anne?'

Was I in any way dishonest?

Back then – and it was only fifteen years ago, but a very different world – it was not possible to be an evangelical and openly gay. Today, post-Vaughan, post-Vicky, it's still hard, but there are more and more of us who will fight for the right to be honestly who we are, and to work with the Scriptures honestly as we are, because this has to be better than the pressure that is placed on gay people when we have to hide.

If I go further back – to when I was a teenager and about to go to university or in my early university years at Oxford – I remember this: I had so many questions. About myself. About other people. About God, and did he love me or hate me. And I couldn't talk to anyone because it was the mid-1980s, and if I told anyone I was gay, all I felt I would get in my evangelical church life was condemnation. I heard everything that was said – by everyone. From the pulpit. From the pews. It made being open impossible.

So life was crushingly lonely.

Well, I have friends from those days who it turns out were also gay – though we didn't know about each other at the time; and some are not in churches any more; and some have just a bit of a link with Christian life; and some are no longer alive. And one or two, through it all, are gloriously wonderful examples of Christian love.

I wish we could have spoken. I wish someone could have spoken to us. I wish someone could have opened the Scriptures to us at that age and showed us how much God loved us. In huge part my motivation for asking the question – is it possible to have a different biblical understanding than that which was given to me when I was such a lonely teenager? – is because I'd love to help young men and women in our churches today not to feel lonely, not to feel as though no one cares, not to think that no one understands, and above all to know beyond doubt that God loves them passionately –

Because the Bible says so.

You need to know this – it's only fair – but this is only fair too: judge what follows not on my starting point or on your reaction to it, but on my handling of Scripture and the fairness of the questions I raise. My journey of faith may well cause me to fall into all kinds of errors – or it may simply make me ask familiar questions differently and therefore freshly, and consequently with a value that may surprise.

Please read, and judge by the content – we evangelicals are people of the Book, not the covers.

CHAPTER ONE

DOES ST PAUL HATE GAYS?

First, let's understand this. The debate on the Scriptures and homosexuality is strangely framed. I don't know why this is. I guess when I first started thinking about this with my theological backstory and the baggage that gives me, I sort of half imagined that the debate must have been started by some scholars in the more liberal wing of the Church with an interest in the social and human stories of faith. They, ever keen to push the Church out of its comfort zone, presented the whole question as working around only the smallest handful of teeny-tiny texts in the whole of the Bible to demonstrate the paucity of scriptural restrictions on the subject. We evangelicals (not being great at this kind of topic, and being a bit wrong-footed when really we are far more interested in writing about Calvin and the Cross or how to evangelise people at work – and also maybe not always being averse to the odd knee-jerk reaction) actually believed that these were the only places where the Bible refers to gay people and replied: 'See – every time the Bible talks about homosexuality it's negative! Therefore, homosexuality must be bad!'

Now I realise that this probably bears no resemblance to reality. I expect what actually happened was far, far stranger. However, if we are going to travel anywhere, I guess we have to start our journey where people usually begin – that handful of teeny-tiny texts. So here goes.

Let's start from the very beginning . . .

The small group of Bible texts commonly used in homosexuality debates in the Church usually comprises: Genesis 19 (the Sodom and Gomorrah story); Leviticus 18:22; Leviticus 20:13; Romans 1:26-27; 1 Corinthians 6:9-11; 1 Timothy 1:9-10; and Jude:7. Three texts in the Old Testament, four in the New. It might be fair to point out that what we see here is that there is a story in the early chapters of Genesis and two references in Leviticus, then apparently nothing in the rest of the Old Testament. In the New Testament we have only four Epistle references. So there is nothing in the Old Testament Prophets, for example. When God's people wandered away and kept abandoning everything God had for them, not a single mention was made of this issue. And there's nothing in the Wisdom literature; not a passing reference in Psalms or Proverbs, nothing about what the wicked or the righteous would do if they faced a gay person by chance late at night and didn't know what kind of drink to order. Nothing, in fact, in the vast majority of the Jewish Bible. And there's nothing in the Gospels either, allowing some to argue that St Paul seems to have a problem that Jesus never mentions. Well, my Bible comes to me as the word of God even when the words aren't in red, so I'm not worried about that line. But the sheer volume of gaps ought to wave a red flag at anyone trying to present this as a major biblical theme.

The thing is, these texts – commonly used as they are in our debates – are rather subjective and most certainly not exhaustive. We get hung up on them because they have been presented to us for some years as the biblical overview, and we have all believed this. Proof-texting any topic may be a decent way to start looking at something, but it's never a decent way to get to the end of a debate. This random handful of verses misses out all sorts of texts the Bible has to offer on the subject. And frankly, a couple of them are extremely arbitrary. There is an element of tilting at windmills in the Sodom story – the sexual element isn't only about homosexual acts; raping young girls is included. Other biblical references find the hospitality question in Sodom to be important while the sexual element seems to be ignored entirely; making the sin of Sodom synonymous with 'sodomy' is unfortunate and perhaps the spirit of previous ages is shaping our reactions here. Jude is also a strange inclusion in the list. ('Strange flesh' in context is indeed a strange phrase, but to make it about gay men may be pushing it and depends upon interpretation as much as translation.) Ian Paul, in his essay 'The Biblical Case for the "Traditional" position' comments: 'None of these texts specify the sin of Sodom as same-sex sexual relations, and modern commentators are right to note that the primary offence was a violent breach of hospitality [. . .] Jude 7 is difficult to interpret; it would be an odd expression for same-sex activity, and perhaps hints at the bizarre idea of having sex with angels.'[12]

Extra baggage for the journey

If we are sticking to simple references, the existence in Old Testament times of male and female shrine prostitutes should be included in any such list of texts. These are often difficult texts for us to understand, often in difficult places in the Scriptures, but basically they refer to dark times in the Old Testament when

---

12. Ian Paul, 'The Biblical Case for the "Traditional" position', in *Grace and Disagreement Part 2. A Reader: Writings to resource conversations*, The Archbishops' Council, 2015.

the people of God did not behave like the people of God. They took on the habits of the nations around them, making altars to local deities in little temples on hillsides and under trees around every village and community. 'Worship' meant having sex there. Texts that look at this explicitly include Deuteronomy 23:17-18 where Israelites are forbidden from taking on this trade and 2 Kings 23:7 where Josiah tears down the dwellings of the male shrine prostitutes that existed even in the Temple of the Lord. And the assumption is that it wasn't women who were having sex with male shrine prostitutes.

Now, this is hardly a positive addition to the list of texts about homosexuality, but it's there, and I think we'll see later that the fuller understanding of these texts gives us a fuller understanding of the more familiar texts that people usually focus on.

Of course, the friendship of David and Jonathan is sometimes cited. This brings up strong reactions. There is a clear divide here: anyone who wants to find positive gay role models in the Scriptures finds 'conclusive' evidence that these two were absolutely involved sexually. Why not? David was clearly a man with voracious sexual appetite. Jonathan risked his life for David. This was some friendship.[13] On the other hand, anyone who wants to preserve traditional understandings of biblical morality equally finds it very clear that the Bible in no way gives any evidence that anything beyond deep friendship was in play. Why do we need to add to the text?

In a similar spirit, Gerd Theissen was the first writer I came across to mention the healing of the centurion's slave in

---

13. 1 Samuel 18 ff.

Matthew 8 in this context.[14] Luke calls the 'servant' a 'doulos', a 'slave'; Matthew calls him a 'pais', which could be a 'boy' or the passive partner in a homosexual relationship. In a military context, the latter is not impossible, and makes sense of a centurion making enough fuss to go see the healer despite the social boundaries that would have been arguing against him doing so for just another slave. It's an interesting cultural call; it's not clear and not obvious from the text alone and yet it's enough to make a familiar story just uncomfortable enough to offer pause for thought – and perhaps brings the matter into the Gospels. Again, scholars on both sides of the argument find and publish 'conclusive' evidence.[15] I think perhaps they find too much.

Shall we go further? Perhaps we ought to probe the nature and cultural role of eunuchs in ancient society. That Ethiopian eunuch that Philip baptises in Acts 8 – why is he so trusted at court with Candace? What was a eunuch? Was there an expectation that sexuality was affected or questionable in some way? Why would a eunuch be thought trustworthy for a ruler – because they were an outcast from society at large? Some see in the Acts 8 account the first example of outreach to someone who is marginalised for gender reasons. Well, perhaps. In the Torah, eunuchs are forbidden to enter the congregation of the faithful;[16] in Isaiah, a time is prophesied when they will be welcome in the Temple, the presence of God.[17] Jesus of course passes a cryptic comment on this in Matthew 19:12:

---

14. Gerd Theissen, *The Shadow of the Galilean*, SCM Press, 1987, p.106.
15. Ian Paul in his blog gives a good example of the arguments here: http://www.psephizo.com/sexuality-2/did-jesus-heal-the-centurions-gay-lover/ For my liking, both sides are overstated. This text offers a hint; no more, no less.
16. Deuteronomy 23:1; try the King James version for a vivid rendering of the text.
17. Isaiah 56:3-5.

'For there are eunuchs who have been so from birth, and there are eunuchs who have been made eunuchs by men, and there are eunuchs who have made themselves eunuchs for the sake of the kingdom of heaven.'[18]

From Torah to Isaiah to Jesus, the story comes to some completion in Acts 8:26-39 with the conversion and baptism of the Ethiopian by Philip. That's some journey. I will return to this later.

Highway or byway?

My point here is this: I actually don't think that homosexuality *per se* is a major biblical theme, but reducing it to a teeny-tiny handful of proof texts is not a helpful way to begin to think about it. Even if we go up from seven to a dozen, my point remains. It's arbitrary, it misses out a wider understanding of God, and it's not how evangelicals do Scripture. Proof texts never prove anything. We are supposed to know the word better than that, and knowing the word better makes us able to join the dots between ideas and themes across the swathe of Old and New Testaments as they point us towards Jesus and help us to grow more like him.

Besides which, we have to acknowledge (the truism) that the Scriptures were written at a time when the concept of sexual orientation was simply not thought of in the terms we use, and so St Paul never writes a sentence that begins: 'Now about those gay people, this is what you should do/think/say . . .' In some senses, using the Bible like this (as so often we do) means

---

18. English Standard Version (ESV).

we are reading about oranges and looking for apples. We can still find fruitful results to our reading, but it will take some care, some work and some prayer.

So as I look at any given passage (and first we are going to look at what St Paul has to say in Romans 1) I am not going to accept a 'proof text' mentality. I would rather gently ridicule that way of thinking as un-evangelical. That's how others think we work, and when we pander to it we are at our very worst. It will not do. God has much more for us than that.

Sticking to the proof texts should quickly show us that the issue of homosexuality is one of the byways of Scripture. But moving on from that way of thinking and looking at the whole counsel of the Bible soon reminds us that a concern with people – all people – and how we treat all people is constantly, permanently, repeatedly one of the highways of God's word for us.

Questioning the questions

If the first problem we face is that the whole debate is strangely framed when it comes to looking at which Scriptures we choose to use, the second problem comes when looking at how we use the Scriptures we have chosen.

It is an evangelical commonplace to say that all the texts about homosexuality within the pages of the Bible describe it negatively. This leads us to the caricature position where people think St Paul hates gays.

What I want to do is look clearly at some of these texts and ask whether they truly say what traditionally we have been told they say. Sure, I do this because I'm hoping there might be some different answers around, but I'm also doing it because it occurs to me that most of the work that's been done in the past has been done by people presuming (actively or passively) that St Paul was going to be fairly hostile to homosexuality, and they found what they expected to find. I had tea one day with a very good friend of mine, a bishop who has the occasional outspoken moment; as I began to speak about what I think St Paul is doing in Romans 1, he interrupted me and said, 'Well, I just think he's wrong.' He presumed Paul was hostile to gays, so that's all he could ever see, and he wasn't interested in hearing anything more. But it's just possible too that the traditionalist agenda, which would never dream of saying St Paul might make a mistake, hasn't always been as fair on the text as it honestly thought it was being.

It's just possible there's something different here.

The first place I'm going to look at is Romans 1, which is the first place most people look at in the New Testament when seeking what the Scriptures have to say. Honestly, there's no way that this is a chapter that can be made to say St Paul affirms gay marriage. Anyone who tells you that is going way beyond the text.

I hope to show, however, that anyone who uses this chapter to say that 'the Bible says homosexuality is bad' is also going way beyond the text.

Romans 1

The verses usually focused on are vv.26-27. Let's be generous and take a look at a slightly larger section. Here are vv.18-32:

[18] For the wrath of God is revealed from heaven against all ungodliness and wickedness of those who by their wickedness suppress the truth. [19] For what can be known about God is plain to them, because God has shown it to them. [20] Ever since the creation of the world his eternal power and divine nature, invisible though they are, have been understood and seen through the things he has made. So they are without excuse; [21] for though they knew God, they did not honour him as God or give thanks to him, but they became futile in their thinking, and their senseless minds were darkened. [22] Claiming to be wise, they became fools; [23] and they exchanged the glory of the immortal God for images resembling a mortal human being or birds or four-footed animals or reptiles.

[24] Therefore God gave them up in the lusts of their hearts to impurity, to the degrading of their bodies among themselves, [25] because they exchanged the truth about God for a lie and worshipped and served the creature rather than the Creator, who is blessed for ever! Amen.

[26] For this reason God gave them up to degrading passions. Their women exchanged natural intercourse for unnatural, [27] and in the same way also the men, giving up natural intercourse with women, were consumed with passion for one another. Men committed shameless acts with men and received in their own persons the due penalty for their error.

[28] And since they did not see fit to acknowledge God, God gave them up to a debased mind and to things that should not be done. [29] They were filled with every kind of wickedness, evil, covetousness, malice. Full of envy, murder, strife, deceit, craftiness, they are gossips, [30] slanderers, God-haters, insolent, haughty, boastful, inventors of evil, rebellious towards parents, [31] foolish, faithless, heartless, ruthless. [32] They know God's decree, that those who practise such things deserve to die – yet they not only do them but even applaud others who practise them.

When I first started thinking about this text, secretly struggling with my own sexuality as a member of an evangelical church, I suppose my understanding went like this:

In the beginning there was the Creation with all things good, and then there was the Fall. People became distanced from God and acted out the results of that broken relationship. We knew who God was, but we chose to worship something else, to leave God behind, and God gave us over to lives that bore the marks of our decisions. It seemed to my younger self that St Paul placed being gay as an aftermath of the Fall. A result of it. This was a life that bore the marks of the decisions of sin in its widest sense. No one was gay in the Garden of Eden. Therefore (following this train of logic through) I thought that, as sexuality along with every other part of life was subject to redemption, in my fallen-ness I should remain celibate as a sign of hope that I could be redeemed in every part of my being.

I no longer see that as being what is said by this passage.

It may actually be a very fair attitude to live by, but it is not conveyed by these words in this passage. I know people – good, honest, impressive, godly people – who would describe themselves as gay (or might prefer 'same-sex attracted') and who hold to the standard of celibacy as being a requirement for all gay Christians; in no way do I belittle their lives and discipleship. For me personally, however, I think this outlook probably came more from the larger worldview that I had gained from my general evangelical upbringing than from anything specifically here in Romans 1. It is of course true that redemption is something that affects every part of our being. Absolutely. I'd add that it is also true that sexuality is as much broken in most heterosexuals as it is in any gay person I have met, and I just don't think any longer that the Bible says the path to healing for everyone, straight or gay, per force lies in celibacy. That's a misunderstanding of what the Bible says about both redemption and about celibacy.

So what then is Romans 1 about?

Idolatry: the heart of sin

Well, here's where I now start:

St Paul states the fundamental sin of the world: it's idolatry. That is to say, we choose to worship someone or something other than the One True God. This breaks the baseline right relationship between humanity and the Creator, which lies at the heart of what St Paul means when he discusses 'righteousness'. Righteousness is primarily about the right relationship we have with God, and that relationship is right when we worship God with heart, soul, mind and strength. Sin is the break, the brokenness, the relationship gone wrong because we stop worshipping God and (with heart, soul, mind and strength) put something else in his place. Sinful moral acts are the results of this break, not the break itself. In essence, chapter one of Romans takes us from the root problem of the world – idolatry – and points toward the effects or fruit of the problem – immorality. In the Christian (and not-so-Christian) West, we have always been far more concerned with immorality than with idolatry; we love to get hot under the collar about this stuff. But the biblical emphasis is always the other way around. St Paul is clear – it is the breaking of relationship with God that leads to immoral acts and social failure, and any solution to immorality and social failure has to recognise the broken relationship with God that lies at the heart of the problem.

Is that clear? Romans 1 is about what's wrong with the world. What's wrong with the world is that we don't worship God with heart, soul, mind and strength. It's not about sex.

There's a lot more in St Paul's words, of course. I'm simply setting a direction of travel.

Now let's add another level which ought to be fairly obvious, but which might be pushing boundaries for some. Whenever I begin to talk Bible and don't simply repeat the traditionalist view (though, of course, that should read 'one of the traditionalist viewpoints' – put two traditionalists in a room, get three opinions . . .) I know that someone is going to label me a 'revisionist', and usually it's not meant entirely kindly.

Well, I love this label. To be a re-visionist, one is trying literally to see something again. To see something that was always there, but which somehow has become difficult to make out clearly. It is always time to peel away the mist of time and culture and expectation and 'see again' in God's word what God always had for us. We are all, always called to be such 're-envisionists', and I love to be gifted with this label – or anything close to it – and I take it as an enormous compliment.

In 2017, the Reformation 500 anniversary year, the #MeToo movement won the *Time Magazine* 'Person of the Year' award, and it seemed that every major organisation from the BBC to Hollywood was being attacked for perpetuating a gender pay-gap. In such a world the simple truth is: re-envisioning biblical truth changes lives.

The Church should always be at the forefront of fighting social injustice. The Church should always be challenging accepted social mores and changing them into something more akin to God's kingdom. The Church should always be standing with those on the fringes of society and giving them a harbour and a home and a place where at last they are seen as fully human, fully loved.

Because if we don't, if we just get comfortable with what we've always done – then forget 'the fringes of society', it turns out that it is only in my own ministerial lifetime that women have attained any kind of parity with men in the Church of England's pastoral ministry, and it's actually since I moved to my current parishes that women have begun to attain that parity in episcopal ministry. The fringes of society? How about half the human race! No matter what large letters St Paul might use to write 'no male or female', our biblical vision has failed badly.

So let's not be afraid to do a little re-envisioning as we consider how God reveals his truth around the whole issue of homosexuality; let's see again the light and the warmth that God's word has always had for those who have felt pushed into the shadows for far too long. St Paul begins clearly. With his background in the Jewish faith as taught by the Pharisees of his day, he forms his argument in Romans around classic Old Testament concepts. He writes consistently as a man born and raised within Jewish faith and culture. He uses the Old Testament scriptures repeatedly (he's already done it ahead of the passage we have before us[19]) and uses the Torah, the Prophets and the Psalms to form his worldview and make his points, referencing Adam,[20] Abraham,[21] Moses[22] and the place of the Old Covenant Israelite people of God[23] in God's continuing purposes. He considers the Temple festivals of the Day of Atonement and the Passover as he talks about the Cross of Christ.[24] And although he often adds in ideas for an audience made up of Gentiles as well as Jews, it is his own people who get the lion's share of his thinking – obviously: this is where he comes from. Without understanding the Old Testament, it is impossible to understand Romans.

Which gives us a problem.

---

19. E.g. Romans 1:17 referencing Habakkuk 2:4.
20. Romans 5:14 ff.
21. Romans 4:1 ff.
22. Romans 10:5 ff – Isaiah, Elijah and David also explicitly feature in Romans 10 and 11.
23. The whole of chapters 9 to 11.
24. Romans 3:22-26: the references are layered; but 'redemption' certainly speaks of Passover, and 'sacrifice of atonement' points to the mercy seat of the Day of Atonement festival.

Separating the sickness from the symptom

Romans 1 deals with idolatry as the fundamental sin of the world. The brokenness of the world is our brokenness from God. That's clear enough. But is this true of all of Romans 1? Or only parts of Romans 1? Which bits say this and which move on from there to how the fundamental sin of the world affects real lives in real places? Does St Paul have one consistent thought here, or does he contradict himself?

Let me put that question another way. Luther had an analogy of the Christ as a doctor, and the gospel as the cure to any person sick with sin. Luther asked: when does the cure begin? His answer (from Romans) was: when the diagnosis is given.

Here's Luther's analogy, talking of a sinner as 'the sick man' and Christ as 'the doctor': 'Now do we say the man who is sick is actually well? In fact, he is both. The man is fatally sick and fighting fit. He is actually sick, but also well because of the sure diagnosis of the doctor, in whom he has faith. This doctor already reckons him as fighting fit, because he is sure that he will cure him, yes – he has already begun to cure him and so does not see the sickness as fatal any more.'[25]

St Paul makes a diagnosis of the problem with the world – that everyone sins and falls short of the glory of God. He begins that story in Romans 1 with a necessary definition of the fundamental sin of the world: worshipping something/anything/everything other than God. That's what Paul means by idolatry.

But – and this is the key question for what follows – how much of Romans 1 is that diagnosis and that definition, and how much simply a commentary on the symptoms?

---

25. The author's own translation and paraphrase of the original German, from Luther's *Lectures on Romans*.

Making use of Luther's analogy, idolatry is obviously the sickness; immorality is the major symptom.

Our problem is this: which is which in Romans 1?

Let's look again at the text.

Accepting that vv.18-23 are clearly about idolatry, people exchanging the glory of God for worthless images, we then get v.24, where we appear to head towards immorality – God giving people over to their sexual lusts. Then we seem to veer back to an idolatry reference in v.25 – indeed perhaps *the* idolatry reference of serving created things rather than the Creator. Verses 26-27 appear to see us moving full force to immorality with the shameful lusts and unnatural relations. Here we go – once people have gone away from worshipping God they head for Capital-I Immorality, and (in a traditionalist reading) St Paul uses as his first, prime, major example of this immorality the issue of homosexuality. As bad as it gets. And then in vv.28-32 he rounds off the chapter by taking us into further areas of social behaviour affected by the fall away from right relationship with God.

So what's the problem?

There are two problems.

First, we know (or think we know) that St Paul can be obtuse and hard work. We expect him to write in a style that is sometimes hard to follow. It doesn't occur to us in our modern vanity that this is the very start of his argument in a long treatise, and that maybe – just maybe – he knew exactly what he was doing and that his first hearers would understand he was making one simple point. At best we sort of work through this with one eye on idolatry, the other on immorality, and when St Paul flips between them, we (just about) keep up. Especially as we are far more concerned with the immorality stuff – which he gets to eventually. But maybe – just maybe – he has different priorities to us, and he's nowhere near as confused in presenting them as we think. (At worst, of course, we are simply using this text as a proof text about sexuality and we have no idea what is really going on here at all – no concept that St Paul isn't writing about that for a moment . . .)

Second: for someone grounded in Jewish scholarship, it's not very Old Testament. I mean, in fact it all feels very modern – our current concerns, our contemporary social issues – we see that if people fall from God then the ultimate result is sexual sin, and chief amongst it – all that gay stuff. But our cultural take blinds us to the simple truth that it's really hard to get this from the Old Testament. If you were starting from the Old Testament and making an argument of a journey from idolatry to immorality, from leaving God to losing everything, and you had to choose your first, prime, major morality issue to put at the height of a piece like this – I don't think homosexuality would even occur to you. Three, maybe four texts in the whole Jewish scriptures? Even scraping around for extras, we are pushed for half a dozen. Certainly not double figures.

If the argument is about idolatry leading to immorality then what about using major Old Testament issues such as oppression of the poor? Adultery? Disobeying parents? Why doesn't St Paul just go there?

Just on numbers of people affected – why go for such a small minority, no matter how bad you thought they were? I remember reading a comment about this on a blog somewhere that said something like: 'The Bible contains 6 admonitions to homosexuals and 362 to heterosexuals. That doesn't mean that God doesn't love heterosexuals. It's just that they need more supervision.' Nicely put. My point here is – gay people just don't get any print space in the Scriptures, whilst straight people are constantly being brought to heel for all their sexual shenanigans.

To make the big argument, surely if St Paul were doing the whole journey from wrong worship to wrong living, and a sexual sin was required to underscore that point, adultery is a huge Old Testament issue and would fit the bill? Or there's plain old generalised prostitution – both of which sins were used as metaphors by the Prophets for the causes of the Exile, that great, disastrous, world-changing turnaround for the Jews six hundred years before Jesus. The whole idolatry to immorality trip is strangely and perversely indicated by St Paul by using homosexuality as his key issue; it just doesn't work in the Bible terms that the rest of his argument depends on. A Jew of his day would frankly look at it and go – 'Huh?'

Or does St Paul really hate gays? And if he does, why shouldn't my outspoken bishop friend be right to say – 'I just think he's wrong'?

Talking about gay sex in this context may look obvious to us, but our contemporary terms are not, I fear, so obvious either to St Paul or to his readers, and that's a huge problem.

Getting the context

I'm afraid this thought occurs to me every time I read excellent books on this topic. For example, Loader's *Sexuality in the New Testament* provides a very thorough run-through of how people in the first century understood sexuality, and how a Jewish audience of St Paul's time would read texts on homosexuality and perceive the matter generally.[26] However, though Loader does refer to the place of idolatry in the argument of Romans 1,[27] he then basically uses the chapter as if it is simply a theological treatise on attitudes to gay people and what they get up to. Given the rest of contemporary literature, Loader has no doubt that Paul is pretty clear that gay sex is not acceptable.

Loader's work is detailed, his understanding of the surrounding literature extremely thorough, and I recommend reading his work – with this caveat: Romans 1 is not about sex and sexuality. And it's certainly not about homosexuality. Any work on Scripture and sexuality has to wrestle with the issue of context because (again) nowhere in the New Testament do we find anyone simply saying, 'Now, about those gay people and what they get up to, this is what you should think.'

Let me repeat that in case you missed it.

Nowhere in the New Testament do we find anyone simply saying: 'Now, about those gay people and what they get up to, this is what you should think.'

Certainly not in Romans 1.

St Paul does not begin his great theological treatise with an issue that would be irrelevant to almost all of his readers/ hearers. He could be obtuse, but not when he wanted to say something that really mattered.

---

26. William Loader, *Sexuality in the New Testament*, SPCK, 2010, chapter 2.
27. Ibid., p.12.

Arguments that try to understand what Romans 1 has to say about the sexuality issue must fail – until, of course, we stop using the proof texts and start getting the context.

Why does St Paul refer to homosexuality in Romans 1?

Understanding why St Paul refers to homosexual behaviour in Romans 1 requires us to understand the journey of the general argument of idolatry to immorality, and to understand both how St Paul shapes that argument – and who his targets are as he speaks.

Let's look at how Paul shapes the argument.

Idolatry and immorality: a journey and souvenirs

Living in the twenty-first century Western world, we are used to a secular society where moral ideas are more important than religious ones. The BBC is stuck in a fairly continuous debate about its Radio 4 'Thought for the Day' slot because, while some people think that religion is more important than ever in a world where being religiously literate matters, others feel that religion is a taint on society. It's a good debate – and it's a change because, twenty years ago, the former group wouldn't have been taken seriously enough to make the debate work! These people are keen not just to have the debate in the public sphere but to make it matter too – because, they say, you can't understand the ethics and behaviour of much of today's wider world without understanding its faith.

Even so, ethics and faith are often presented as sometimes overlapping but by no means interdependent realities. Sure, if you choose faith then that may lead to a certain ethic, a set of moral values (usually viewed as 'conservative' – especially in America or, ironically, the Middle East) but choosing not-faith doesn't mean the absence of an ethical standard. It means a different journey. A different destination. There may well be lots of common factors; but there will also be clear points of distinction.

This modern worldview inevitably affects us when we read St Paul. We see he has a religious understanding that sets up his moral ethic. But as we look deeper at that religiously based moral ethic, to be frank, St Paul can seem confused . . .

When we read St Paul we have to let go of our own context and understand that, not only for St Paul but for his whole world, life worked differently. The road from worship to ethics, idolatry to immorality was not a journey like that from England to France – twenty miles of clear water between the two, without any doubt as to which country you might be in at any time. It was much more like travelling along the Welsh Marches: you endlessly greet the 'Croeso i Gymru' signs, and realise that, with the rolling hills and bending road, you have been continually swapping between England and Wales without noticing. The border between the two is complicated and interlocking and now – as in ages past – it means that the two countries seamlessly belong together, affecting each other in all sorts of ways. Journeying from one to the other is not always a simple thing – sometimes it even feels like you are in them both at the same time. If you can grasp this about Romans 1, the argument remains solidly on Old Testament terms.

How come?

There is no straight-line journey from idolatry to immorality in Romans 1. The two concepts are not separate, with clear blue water between them. They are interlinked. One may be a larger territory; but they shape each other.

In order to see homosexuality in Romans 1 purely as an immorality issue, and therefore as an issue that has some relevance to the secular societal issue we think we recognise and face today, we presume St Paul gets a bit sloppy in his writing. We're stuck on Eurostar, criss-crossing the Channel as Paul swaps between the England and France of idolatry and immorality from moment to moment: vv.21-23 are clearly about the fundamental sin of idolatry – actually expressing it in terms of making idols. Then in v.24, St Paul gets ahead of himself and starts talking about sexuality as immorality ('Therefore God gave them up in the lusts of their hearts to impurity, to the degrading of their bodies among themselves'), before realising he's not finished on idolatry, which he does in v.25 ('they exchanged the truth about God for a lie and worshipped and served the creature rather than the Creator'). Having done that, he can really let rip in vv.26-27: because people have abandoned the worship of God, God has given them over to sexual perversion. That's the big immorality sin. And it's followed in vv.28-31 with other social sins that also happen.

But what if that's not what's going on? What if it's not St Paul's thinking that's sloppy, but ours?

Change the location back: what if he's just driving along the Welsh Marches, driving one road that effortlessly slips between two linked territories, with one fundamental landscape revealed by the other – and the fundamental landscape is not the one we usually focus on? What if St Paul is in fact living in an intellectual framework where worship and its opposite – idolatry – is the major issue, and where the height of idolatry is given to him by the writers of the Old Testament, and not just by his imagination? What if that means the practice of idolatry and sexual excess (in every form) are inextricably linked – like a border road that keeps dipping between two states, revealing all with every rising contour of the land?

For us this is hard to grasp. We continually fail to grasp how big a deal idolatry is in the Scriptures. And actually, whilst idolatry undoubtedly follows through to immorality in Paul's thinking, the 'journey' metaphor only gets us so far. Wrong worship is the whole journey in itself. It doesn't take us anywhere other than away from God. It is its own end. When we have chosen it, we have already arrived. All that is left to do is buy the souvenirs, wear the T-shirt. Then everyone can tell where we've been.

How?

Grasping an Old Testament worldview

Let's start with the Old Testament.

For the Hebrew people of God, first occupying Canaan under Joshua in the days after Moses, things looked rather different. The laws of Leviticus 18 and 20 (where we find two of our original handful of proof texts about homosexuality) place a number of sexual practices out of bounds for God's people – principally because they break the God/people worship relationship, not just because they're what we would view as being 'morally wrong'. The Canaanite god Molech even gets a name-check in the process. Both of these Leviticus chapters are topped and tailed by warnings for God's people not to live like the people around them for reasons of relationship – of keeping worship right with God:

> Speak to the people of Israel and say to them: I am the Lord your God. You shall not do as they do in the land of Egypt, where you lived, and you shall not do as they do in the land of Canaan, to which I am bringing you. You shall not follow their statutes. My ordinances you shall observe and my statutes you shall keep, following them: I am the Lord your God. (Leviticus 18:2-4)

I am the Lord your God. Worship me; stay with me; be faithful to me. Don't worship the local deities – in whatever remarkable ways the natives get up to.

This wasn't a general secularist moral plea or a narrow call for intolerance. Ancient Canaanite poems, the local love songs of the day, are full of sexual excess in the context of religious practice, and the purity of Hebrew religious practice (bluntly – no sex in church) was in sharp contrast to it. The Israelites weren't just trying to be better than their neighbours, or stricter or more straight-laced – that's a modern and unspiritual society's anachronistic reading of these texts. I sat with a head teacher from a school a few miles away from my home recently who was distressed that our diocese places terrific importance on the 'ethos' of church schools. She complained – 'Don't they realise we all want our children to be nice to each other!' Well, we do; but as I sat there, I rather felt that this was exactly why our church schools place such an importance on their ethos: precisely because our ethos is about so much more than 'being nice'.

The Old Testament people of God didn't have a life where morality was divorced from spirituality, as we experience in modern Britain. Rather, God's people were not to indulge in the excesses they found amongst the peoples they met on their journeys because those excesses came from a worship life that was far from the worship life they were called to. Leviticus 18 begins with the statement 'I am the Lord' repeated, and repeated again, and again.

If you go on a journey of worship, your life will show where you have been. Right worship, wrong worship, you choose. And in doing so, you choose what souvenirs of the journey you bring home with you. You bear the fruit of your choices.

How you worship shows who you worship. It's who you worship that matters.

The descriptions of abandoning God and of various kinds of sexual excess in Romans 1 are all about how people worshipped. They're about what worship looks like because that shows who and what you have chosen to put in God's place. And who and what you have chosen to put in God's place shapes who and what you are – and what you do. The fruit of your choices. The souvenirs of your journey.

If you have chosen to worship God, who is faithful and true, you will lead a life of faithfulness and truth in all your relationships. If you choose to put pleasure or 'the moment' in that place then you will live out the implications of that worship choice. These days, we're told 'we are what we eat': the Bible ups the stakes. 'We become what we worship.' If you want different souvenirs, choose a different shop.

If just something of this is in St Paul's mind then vv.24-28 are not muddled verses, flicking between idolatry and immorality as Paul forgets himself and goes back and restates his case, they belong just as they are. We become who we worship, so choose carefully – except the choice has been made, and it wasn't careful. We shopped cheaply. Fallen humanity, says St Paul, exchanged the worship of God for the worship of idols – and in practice that worship involved sexual excess of all and every kind. And people became what they chose.

Rotten fruit.

St Paul is very, very clear about this. Three times he writes: 'God gave them up': in v.24 'in the lusts of their hearts to impurity'; in v.26 'to degrading passions'; and in v.28 'to a debased mind and to things that should not be done'. God allowed them to behave like the false gods they worshipped. Truth gave way to a lie, worshipping the Creator was swapped for worshipping something created. And in those shameful revels, done in the name of religion, in the name of worship, people kept debasing themselves in a spirit of 'anything goes'. This didn't involve love, or faithfulness, or the mutual relationship of equals seeking to find a life partner – this was wantonness and orgy and promiscuity gone mad. In the name of religion, in the name of worship. Humanity forgetting itself.

An agenda of life for everyone

It's not a question of straight and gay – every excessive behaviour is condemned in these passages. It's a question of who is God, and what is God like, and also – how God's agenda shapes the lives of those who follow him.

If you worship pleasure, who should trust you? Faithfulness is fleeting, at best a means to an end, no longer the certain bedrock of life.

Seeing how St Paul shapes his argument gives us a far better chance of understanding who his targets are.

Is St Paul thinking of a tiny group of gay men in some seedy bar in ancient Rome as he writes of 'degrading passions' and 'shameless acts' in Romans 1? No – St Paul is describing every Jew's (at least of his period) caricature of the entire idolatrous Gentile world. It's ancient Egypt, ancient Canaan, it's Babylon, it's Corinth, it's certainly Rome. They're all at it.

This is broken Gentile worship. This is the whole broken Gentile world. Or at least it is a polemic, hyperbolic version of it. In Old Testament terms, this is what we see in places like Deuteronomy 23:18 – which I mentioned earlier. In Deuteronomy, the earnings of a shrine prostitute may not be used to pay a vow in the Temple. The word for 'male shrine prostitute' is actually 'dog', a reference often taken as referring to sexual position. The term 'dog' as a Jewish expression of contempt for Gentiles and the godless generally can be found throughout the Scriptures.[28] It is used by Jesus in Matthew 15. It describes those locked outside the New Jerusalem at the end of the biblical witness.[29] Deuteronomy 23 gives a strong case for its root – it's a sexual slander. A dog is an idolater who knows no limits to their excess. A person – quite possibly in our terms a straight person, for the Bible writers know only of the actions of passion and not of

---

28. Psalm 22:16, for example.
29. Revelation 22:15.

orientation – who, in the frenzy of pagan worship, loses their identity. St Paul describes this person in Romans 1:27.

So Romans 1 isn't a passage that says: Now about those gay people, this is what you should think.

But it does say: Now about those folk that abandon themselves to putting anything and everything other than God first in their lives, and specifically about those Gentiles who have never belonged to God's people, this is what you should think:

> [29] They were filled with every kind of wickedness, evil, covetousness, malice. Full of envy, murder, strife, deceit, craftiness, they are gossips, [30] slanderers, God-haters, insolent, haughty, boastful, inventors of evil, rebellious towards parents, [31] foolish, faithless, heartless, ruthless. [32] They know God's decree, that those who practise such things deserve to die – yet they not only do them but even applaud others who practise them.

This is the world St Paul attacks. This is his target. This is the broad brush that paints the town red, and which covers all the pride of the Gentiles in unwashable shame. It's not about sex.

So it's St Paul against the world then?

It's not about sex.

And – equally – it's not about sects. Having set up such an extreme view of the rest of the world, of course, Paul quickly slams down any Jewish pride or feeling of one-upmanship over their Gentile neighbours in Romans 2:1: 'Therefore you have no excuse, whoever you are, when you judge others; for in passing judgement on another you condemn yourself, because you, the judge, are doing the very same things.'

He goes on to drive this home – the Jews are just as guilty, with all their Law and Temple and sacrifices of idolatry, as these Gentile dogs, as guilty of immorality, as guilty of unrighteousness – 'since all have sinned and fall short of the glory of God' (Romans 3:23). That's the point. There isn't one prime, major, overarching moral sin because there *is* one prime, major, overarching spiritual sin. Everyone is as guilty as everyone else. St Paul starts with stunning images of excess and the loss of humanity, in order to show that true sin, that broken relationship from God, the absence of 'righteousness', that choice to worship someone or something other than the Creator means we all lose our humanity. We are all in this together. (I will come back here, later.)

St Paul hates gays? On the evidence of Romans 1, he barely gives them the time of day. And if he does – it's because he calls on everyone who gives their heart to someone or something other than God to realise what that choice has done. And to realise there is more, far more, open to us by God's great love and kindness.

It's All About Worship

We have been looking at St Paul's words in Romans 1 because they are often a starting point for traditionalist arguments that the Bible sees homosexuality as bad. My contention is that a serious look at that passage just doesn't support that viewpoint. By no means can anyone twist the text to have St Paul say 'Gays are great' – but he doesn't say the opposite either. It's just not what he's talking about.

His first concern is always what the Bible's first concern is – worship, and the right worshipping relationship of people to God.

We look at Romans 1 and Paul's talk of exchanging the natural for the unnatural and presume he's laying down a general moral line when he hasn't got anywhere near it: he's got far more important things to talk about, and it's our paucity of biblical understanding that wants to rush past the question of idolatry to the really juicy stuff. This is the juicy stuff. And it's not focused on what people do to each other with their bodies – what they do with their bodies comes from what they are doing with their hearts.

Fruit of the journey.

Sure, Paul speaks of sexual activity in the context of idolatry, but to divorce activity from context and then make blind moral judgements that have no reference to the original context is to cherry-pick Scripture and should be looked at with great scepticism by any serious disciple. Romans 1 is not there simply to answer our contemporary questions of straight and gay, of equal marriage, or how a church should react to two Christian folk of the same gender who love each other and want to devote their lives to one another. Personally, I've never been asked, 'I'm considering devoting my life to pleasure and want to know whether the Bible minds if, as I give myself to whatever comes along, I use my body to reflect that spiritual search and basically, you know, sleep with anything that moves?'

Though, put like that, it does sound pretty contemporary.

Mind you, if I was asked that question, I could answer it really clearly from Romans 1 – and, even more, from Romans 12.

Romans 12: Worship that makes sense

If there were any doubt about the point of the homosexual language in Romans 1, St Paul himself makes it clear where he is coming from when he reverses the mess of chapter 1 with the glory of chapter 12. As evangelicals, when we are unclear what the Bible is saying, the way we interpret the Scriptures is by using the Scriptures. Proof texts prove nothing; the whole counsel of Scripture does not depend upon our feelings or our culture or our need for it to say something. The Scriptures make the Scriptures plain.

If I was asked that question about someone devoting their life to pleasure, and all that follows on from that search, like any good evangelical I'd head to Romans 12. It's not about sexuality, it's not about sex, it's about worship. We are made to devote ourselves to God, with all that follows on from that search. Worshipping something else, some other created thing, leads us spiritually downward, no matter how good it feels; giving ourselves to God allows Christ to raise us up. We will always carry home the souvenirs of whichever of these journeys we have chosen to take.

The right way up

The opening to Romans 12 finds the relationship between God and humanity gloriously restored and turns the right way up all that was spoiled in Romans 1:

> I appeal to you therefore, brothers and sisters, by the mercies of God, to present your bodies as a living sacrifice, holy and acceptable to God, which is your spiritual worship. Do not be conformed to

> this world, but be transformed by the renewing of your minds, so that you may discern what is the will of God – what is good and acceptable and perfect. (Romans 12:1-2)

In Romans 1, we had 'the wrath of God [being] revealed', and because of our sin 'God gave [us] up' to the results of our choices. But in Romans 12 this is transformed and there is a different revelation; now we live 'by the mercies of God'.

In Romans 1 we dwelt in a world where simply existed 'all the ungodliness and wickedness of [people]', but now in Romans 12 we have been amazingly transformed into people 'holy and acceptable to God'.

This has happened because the darkening of 'senseless minds' where we 'became fools' as we exchanged the worship of the Creator for the worship of any created thing in Romans 1 has gloriously been turned around in Romans 12 by our 'spiritual worship' – or, better, a 'reasonable' act, *logikén* worship, worship that replaces foolishness with something that really makes sense.

In Romans 1, it was the common condition 'not to acknowledge God' and to sink into the life that happens as a result of not acknowledging him; in Romans 12 something wonderful has happened: we will not 'be conformed to this world' because, although in Romans 1 we were given 'up to a debased mind', in Romans 12 we have been 'transformed by the renewing of [our] minds'.

So we have been rescued from living a life in Romans 1 where '[We] know God's decree, that those who practise such things deserve to die – yet [we] not only do them but even applaud others who practise them'; now, in Romans 12, we have wonderfully become those able to 'discern what is the will of God – what is good and acceptable and perfect'.

The reversal of the brokenness of Romans 1 with the right relationship of Romans 12 is one of the rhetorical glories of the book, and the only problem with it is this: if we accept a traditionalist use of St Paul with the movement from idolatry to immorality relying on his prime illustration of the evils of gay sex in Romans 1, straight sex just doesn't figure in his correction of the world gone wrong in Romans 12. Everything else is reversed. But not that. It's curiously absent.

Now I've stopped at v.2 of Romans 12. I should go on: in vv.9-21 Paul is going to begin the picture of how right relationship with God transforms right relationship with each other, talking about what the fruit of *this* journey looks like by contrast with the one he began with in Romans 1. And even here, even when he gets into all sorts of detail on the souvenirs we find from the greatest Gift shop ever, there is never a transformation of homosexual transgression into anything 'redeemed'. It doesn't happen. Not a whisper.

What does happen, however, is what I have left out. I hope you noticed it. For I have missed out perhaps the most famous words from Romans 12:1. They are the reversal of the homosexual references in Romans 1. They use the same language:

> 'I appeal to you therefore, brothers and sisters, by the mercies of God, to present your bodies as a living sacrifice.'

To present, to offer your bodies as a living sacrifice.

Living Sacrifices: Living Worship

In Romans 1, all that we so often see as simple moral perversion is not about sex, it's about idolatry and the results of idolatry on people's lives. It's the breaking of relationship with God and the worship of anything else that comes from that which St Paul is still talking about, and the reversal of it in Romans 12 makes this clear. In Romans 1:22-24 we get: 'they became fools; and they exchanged the glory of the immortal God for images resembling a mortal human being or birds or four-footed animals or reptiles. Therefore God gave them up in the lusts of their hearts to impurity, to the degrading of their bodies among themselves.' The degrading of their bodies in the place of worship – which now, in Romans 12, becomes the offering of our bodies in the place of worship as living sacrifices, sacrifices that bring life, not take it away as in Romans 1.

Romans 1:25-27 follows straight away with the same idea repeated: 'They exchanged the truth about God for a lie and worshipped and served the creature rather than the Creator, who is blessed for ever! Amen. For this reason God gave them up to degrading passions', and that's where we read the specifically homosexual language.

'Their women exchanged natural intercourse for unnatural, and in the same way also the men, giving up natural intercourse with women, were consumed with passion for one another. Men committed shameless acts with men and received in their own persons the due penalty for their error.'

But context rules: we are people of the Book, not of the covers, and we don't skim the surface of the Scriptures in order to get them to agree with us. We work harder than that. Cut out of context, printed all by themselves, these two verses of St

Paul do make him sound a tad homophobic. He's not. This is not about homosexuality, it's about idolatry and the acts that make all of us lose our humanity as we have lost our relationship with God, and this is the deep, great, primary sin that gets reversed so that all the other sinful things all of us have in our lives can be addressed.

Having spent two verses, two glorious verses, at the start of Romans 12 encapsulating the whole problem of Romans 1 and showing how Christ sets us free to live as we should and not in the mess the world places before us, St Paul adds an extra dimension as he continues. He has talked about the offering of our bodies not as pagan excess but as worship that makes sense, and then goes from 'our bodies' to the 'one body'. This stunning reversal of Romans 1 shows how completely the language of that chapter was never to be read as a focused ethic of the few, but as an encapsulation of the brokenness of each and every one of us: 'For as in one body we have many members, and not all the members have the same function, so we, who are many, are one body in Christ, and individually we are members one of another (Romans 12:4-5).

Life, and its goals – true worship – is not to be focused in sensual selfishness but in self-offering and service. This is the opposite of idolatry. This is life in all its fullness. It is for everyone, every person, all who call upon the name of the Lord, and all are needed, valued, loved and find belonging in this glorious body where Christ himself is the head.

Please, how can this ever be a response to mere homosexuality? The Body of Christ is hardly reserved for reformed gays! We know and trust and rejoice that this is where all humanity finds its truest home.

CHAPTER TWO

PEOPLE ARE HUMAN

Recap: as an evangelical and as a gay man, I want to be able to open my Bible and talk to others with open Bibles without there being no-go areas. I want to be able to disagree with traditionalist, conservative takes on sexuality without calling other people homophobes and without them doubting my commitment to Christ. I don't want or need everyone to agree with me; though that would be nice for them . . . And I really don't want the Church I belong to and love to split because people who are actually my friends think I'm worth splitting the Church over.

Seriously, I'm not worth splitting the Church over.

So I want to find a way of looking at the Scriptures that is fair and biblical, and which lets those who disagree with me understand that we have the same heart and follow the same Lord.

We just disagree. Sometimes quite strongly. But I hope we're trying (in Archbishop Justin Welby's wonderful phrase) to disagree well.

Disagreeing, well . . .

We evangelicals are supposed to be people of the Book – the whole Book. Not just a text here or there. When we formulate theologies and ethics, especially important and restrictive ones on limited parts of Scripture, it can never be enough to say: 'Of course, the Bible says homosexuality is bad – all the texts about it say the same thing.' We might just be reading all those limited references out of their proper context, or failing to translate them fairly into our own context. When I talk about Romans 1, I hope I am never trying to water down the text or wriggle out of plain truth. I honestly believe I'm offering a good, sound, reasonable way of looking at a Scripture that does not actually lead to the conclusion 'homosexuality is bad' because it takes seriously the bigger picture of what the words are saying and how St Paul uses them to draw that bigger canvas. St Paul's point is about idolatry; he cares passionately that people's hearts are broken away from God's. One of his illustrations within that is a specific use of sexuality that doesn't quite fit our common reference.

And yet my personal bigger issue remains this: I don't want or need everyone to agree with me. That would require some pretty selfish and arrogant defining of 'church' or 'truth' on my part. What I do ask is that (agree or not) we develop our positions not on the basis of party line or presumption or prejudice, but on Scripture. I'm happy to talk Scripture, and when I understand I'm in the wrong I'm more than happy to change and to do better. But where we just disagree – then let us have the possibility of difference here as evangelicals, as we do on every other secondary issue under the sun. Adiaphora. The 'big house'. And let's demonstrate a kind and godly generosity to accept each other as loved by God and being people of good heart who desire to serve him.

Friendly fire

Every gay person in the Church has stories of how they have been hit by prejudice. For years I hid in plain sight – I worked really hard to ensure that people had no idea that I was gay. A few very close friends knew. Just because I'm a single bloke, some always wondered, but I was very, very good at the smokescreen. It's true I went to the opera (cliché or what?) but I also went to Old Trafford. I'm one of the few people I know who has actually travelled abroad to a World Cup. That kind of thing stops most people wondering.

And that 'hiding in plain sight' means through those years I heard every single prejudiced thing that gets said in the Church about gay people. Because no one thought not to say it near me. I felt the friendly fire.

One time, I was at theological college and we had to do a study week away from college. I guess it was a time when I was struggling with my sexual identity and, if I'm honest, I really did not want to be away with a group of (almost all) lads, participating in 'banter'. Anyway, on the first day, as we travelled somewhere, one guy (now a terrific evangelist, whom I have always respected) threw out a line – I can't even recall it – but a line that in some way cheaply demeaned gay people. I'm afraid I couldn't take it and I couldn't respond. There were other comments too. It was simply too much.

Later in the day I slipped away from the group, left the study week behind and went home. I couldn't say anything to anyone. Was I too sensitive? Probably. But it was what it was. I was who I was.

A year later, my college principal called me into his office. He told me that he didn't feel able to recommend me for ordination because of one or two elements on my report. He particularly cited my absence without explanation from that study week.

So, for the first time, I told him. I told him the struggle I was going through all by myself. I told him who I was inside. I told him what happened that day on that study week and how it was fairly typical and that there were times when I just couldn't handle it.

My college principal was Dick France. Scholar and author, R. T. France. He became more than a college principal, he became a friend, a dear friend, to me that day and he remained so till he died many years later. I provided one of the national newspapers with a photo for his obituary.

Dick listened, and by his words and his compassion he showed he understood how I felt. And I listened to him and understood that the people who said the things that tore me apart weren't bad people and weren't doing it on purpose. They didn't mean to hurt. It didn't stop the hurt, but it did help the forgiving, and it did help the not-holding-on-to-it.

Learning, listening, loving

Most prejudice doesn't come from wickedness. It comes from not knowing or not understanding. In the Church we have to see this; we have to avoid becoming enemies when Christ died that we might be friends. We have to learn what we don't know, and understand what is beyond us. We have to love – when it's easy, and when it costs.

We have to.

Now it's one thing to look at these Bible texts and find that perhaps they don't clearly say what we thought they clearly said. But what is there in the Scriptures to help us move on from there?

What do the Scriptures give us to help us tackle questions about being gay and being Christian, if places like Romans 1 don't have any easy answers for us?

Early on I said I would add two things at the end of my examination of Romans 1. Here's the first: I think that there is a misconception going on amongst traditionalists that if we evangelicals accept any part of the gay plea to be heard, we have to accept the whole nine yards. This is sometimes referred to as the 'slippery slope' argument, and it says that if you listen to a 'reasonable' gay voice first, the next thing you know there'll be queers marrying in every church and cavorting in bishops' palaces and forcing you to agree it's all good – or else.

I might gently reply: not all heterosexual people are good. Yet clearly we agree God loves people. Perhaps especially the ones in severe need – sinners (I'm recalling Jesus saying something about it being the sick who need a doctor). Likewise, not all gay people are good. And yet God loves us. And not all gay people are extreme. Gay people are as varied as it is possible to be, and a blanket rejection is as ridiculous as blanket approval. Just because something or someone is gay doesn't make it or them right or wrong. That's not the point, though it feels like it has somehow become the point.

So what is the point I am trying to make?

Gay People Are Human

Gay people are human.

The Bible does not demonise any single class of humanity.

No better, no worse

Anyone is intrinsically as sinful as the rest of humanity and no better and no worse. In as much need of forgiveness and redemption, and as capable of standing under grace. Or of missing it.

Think of it this way: King David covets another man's wife, commits adultery and arranges murder, and then repents and sees the child of that adultery die.[30] We know his repentance is real – we read the agony of Psalm 51. Of course, he then still takes Bathsheba for his own and has another son who becomes his preferred heir – preferred above the sons of his previous marriages with Michal,[31] Ahinoam, Abigail, Maacah, Haggith, Abital and Eglah.[32] I'm just saying. This man after God's own heart, held up as the ideal, has apparently been living in something approaching open polygamy. And yet there is in our day a blind eye turned to King David, while by contrast we suffer an open and public ecclesiastical aversion to two men or two women falling in love and wanting to spend their lives together in exclusive faithfulness – like that would be worse, though the Scriptures never actually address such a situation.

But I'm not asking for a judgement call on better or worse here – please listen to this carefully.

People are human. We are not called upon to make public (or private) pronouncements that anyone is better or worse than anyone else. We are the same. Vulnerable. Sinful not primarily for moral reasons but because we live in broken relationship with God. The Bible doesn't shy away from our moral brokenness and

---

30. 2 Samuel 11.
31. 1 Samuel 18.
32. 2 Samuel 3.

mess. And it doesn't condemn us for the brokenness and mess or lock us up into prisons of unbearable lifestyle options as a result. But it does cut to the heart of the real issue and give that far greater import.

A woman, a well, some water and some worship

Take the woman at the well in John 4. Jesus positions himself at Jacob's well at midday. A lonely place, a place where he can have a little down-time while the rest of the gang go get lunch in town. And this woman, this Samaritan woman, comes up to draw water. In the heat of the day – a time when no one in their right mind would come. Unless they had no option. Unless they were forced to come to use the well when no other women would be there.

So Jesus talks to her. A man talking to a woman he doesn't know, a Jew talking to a Samaritan, trampling down every acceptable social barrier. She's reluctant to answer at first, but he pulls her in with a promise of water that never runs dry, a spring she can tap into that means she can drink and drink and it's not like this well that she has to keep coming to every day at midday when no one else is out, every day in the heat of the day, every day reminding her of what she has done and how she is seen and condemned by everyone else.

She wants this water.

'Go bring your husband, we'll talk more,' says Jesus, looking her in the eye, gently. She's taken aback. 'I haven't got a husband,' she replies, just faltering a little. Jesus smiles. 'I know, dear;

you've had five, and the bloke you're with now, well, he's not exactly yours, is he?'

How many of us would do that? And doing it, manage it without one drop of condemnation or judgement? Not one drop – if that had been there, she'd have been off. She got it every day from everybody else. They all know. That's why she was there when she was there. Just verses before this, an essential part of Jesus' manifesto is revealed in John 3:17 – 'Indeed, God did not send the Son into the world to condemn the world, but in order that the world might be saved through him.' It's possible this whole encounter is a real-life working out of that manifesto, a live-action parable of words his disciples needed to see as well as hear, words this woman was desperate to know. Saving not condemning. So Jesus goes on to talk of worship, the restoration of the right relationship with God that lies at the heart of her brokenness, true worship and right relationship which does not lie in places or acts but in spirit and truth and which he is offering to her. There and then.

This restoration, this healing of the fundamental human brokenness goes beyond the morality we get hung up on but which is only at most a sign of the deeper truth. Jesus refers to the surface, kindly, but then takes her to her heart. And as they carry on talking, as she goes and comes back and as her whole community see the Saviour through his 'knowing everything [she] ever did' but not damning her one little bit, people are saved. And you know, there's not one mention of Jesus telling the woman to leave the man who isn't hers. Not one mention of him cleaning up her sexual mess. Not one instruction crossing his lips about how she should behave better, be more upright, get the rules clearer in her head, not screw up.

We can interpolate that stuff, because we feel it should be there – but it is not. Rather we need to be careful when reading these stories and wanting to put some nice moralism in there, because the Bible does not make any one of us the world's moral scapegoat and it would be simply wonderful if we in the Church would consistently remember this.

Offer grace

I mean *remember* this. Forgetting it risks creating an underclass of humanity. There are too many young women and men in the world and in the Church today struggling with their sexual identity, and evangelicals ought to be there to offer them grace. Instead, in direct opposition to Jesus' example and to a text like John 3:17 (saving, not condemning) we often (and from the best motives, I have no doubt, and bearing in mind the words I heard that day from Dick France, often without any intent or even understanding of what we are doing) offer judgement, and these people don't just see us, but because of us they see Jesus pushing them away. I find this unbearable. If the Scripture clearly allowed for any one group of people to become such a moral underclass, it might be forgivable of us to act like this – though it would be a strange exception to the rest of the gospel message. But my suspicion is that culture and a natural heterosexual distrust of homosexuality (and it is natural – a majority always distrusts a different minority) have led over the years to a blindness on this subject which truly has made this a justice issue, and has brought us to a time when justice needs to be served.

I need to pause a moment. I said something that I need to clear up. I used the phrase 'moral underclass' – and I want to be clear what I meant by that. I don't want to use potentially provocative phraseology for the sake of it, or to score cheap points. The point I'm looking for here is that (without thinking, without meaning, and aiming at a higher goal) our words on these subjects can become barriers. They exclude. They come from hearts that mean to invite people through the gates of heaven, but the words themselves are padlocked gates. When we forget ourselves and let even a whiff of moral condemnation enter our conversations, people get locked out of heaven because the tone of our moralistic debates suggests some folk are not good enough for God.

All the detail is then irrelevant. We have created a moral underclass. People not fit for Jesus. And we wonder why they won't be our friends . . .

I'm going to give an example of what I'm talking about in a moment – an example of language that gets used in almost every church. Language that gets used by people who are genuinely trying to do well in these conversations, but that – when you are on the receiving end of it – can leave you feeling like a second-class human being. I have no doubt that very few people who use the example I am about to give ever use it wanting to create that effect. I have every confidence that most would be horrified that this could be the result of their words.

And this is what I mean by being careful. Very few people consciously see gays as being slightly less human. Yet very many gays in the Church have felt they were being seen that way.

Here's my illustration, my example, the phrase you will know very well. Let me go back to the lessons I learned as I spoke all those years ago with Dick France, my college principal. Sometimes good people do not know the effect of what they do or say. When you have felt the rough side of it, you know. A popular line in sexuality debates amongst evangelicals is 'hate the sin, love the sinner'.

That's my example. That line.

Hate the sin, love the sinner.

The truth is that this line can be received as a devastating condemnation, no matter how well-meant it is offered. I know many straight people who would embrace this saying about things they have done, but few who would say it simply of a straight person just because they were straight. It gets said to gay people in the Church just because they're gay. And we are made to feel like sinners on a very special level.

May I say, having sex with another bloke isn't the only thing that makes you gay? If it were, I'd be straight. That line ('love the sinner . . .') sometimes cuts deep because of the implications of just how specially sinful I am as a gay man, and those cuts are the wounds of discrimination, right there. Gay people are (as I say – unintentionally) presented as especially, intrinsically, differently sinful. Any moral line can be subtle and yet felt very, very keenly by those who find themselves stranded on the wrong side. Judgement does not need a courtroom. The unthinking, unintended, often smiling ignorance of the majority is all that's needed.

Besides – hate the sin, love the sinner? What is the sin here – two blokes having sex? Seriously, when did you last see that happening in church? Or are we talking about two guys flirting? Two women holding hands? Or someone getting enthusiastic about Queer Eye season two on Netflix?

When the best that is offered feels like gay people are being asked to look as much like straight folk as possible, and showing any outward signs of being gay might bar someone from the idea of responsibility in the Church, then we are not all equally human. 'People look at the outward appearance, but the Lord looks at the heart,' says God to the prophet Samuel.[33] Nowadays, we like the heart to be kind of sorted, but (oh boy!) the Church is fixated with the outward appearance. Rule number one: Blend in! Even if it makes you ill! Gay people are discouraged from being visible, never mind the basic life experiences that everyone else gets to enjoy and endure – and on what basis?

A venerable misapplication of the text. From time to time in the Church's history such misreadings have had to be dealt with. I've said I quite enjoy the 'revisionist' label – or 're-envisionist', as I think of it – though I understand it isn't always meant kindly. Part of my enjoyment comes because I ask – what is the alternative? That the church community kindly, with what it intends to be genuinely good intentions, continues to allow a whole class of people to remain a little less human than everyone else? The moral underclass, knocking on the padlocked gates of heaven. Of course, it's usually unintentionally done; please realise, of course it's also usually devastating.

Crumbs of love

How devastating? This issue comes through the Scriptures – for example, in the story of the visit of the Canaanite woman in Matthew 15.[34] I'm using this version of this story because of

---

33. 1 Samuel 16:7, New International Version (NIV).
34. Matthew 15:21-28.

Matthew's description of the woman (Canaanite), and because of his description of how she approaches Jesus.

The Leviticus laws against homosexuality are written, in context, in passages that command the Israelites not to be like the people amongst whom they will settle – the Canaanites.[35] They must not accept their morality, which comes from their religious practices which seem to have been on the wild side. They needed the warning: shrine prostitutes (as in Deuteronomy) were most likely an example of an import into the life of God's people from early Canaanite religion.

Now here in Matthew 15 we have a Canaanite woman making a fuss, pleading for mercy, and Jesus apparently ignoring her. He is – I think – intently watching how his disciples respond to the awkward situation.

The disciples' first reaction is to urge Jesus to send the woman away. Stop the fuss. Restore order. She's a nuisance. A woman breaking into the men's company, a woman speaking out of turn, a foreigner defiling Jewish purity – does she have no manners at all? Canaanites. What do you expect? No one suggests he help her. And I wonder if Jesus' answer at this point is to the disciples, not to the woman – they, after all, are the ones who have spoken to him.

'Hmm,' he says to them, raising an eyebrow, 'send her away as a way of dealing with her? After all, I'm only here for God's beloved, right?'

Good people sometimes do not know the effect of casual words and actions. The disciples were not being intentionally cruel. However, when you have felt the rough side of those casual words and actions, you know it. This woman knows it.

---

35. Leviticus 18:22; 20:13.

And now feeling everything, she does something extraordinary: Matthew says she worships Jesus. (Verse 25 – 'knelt'[36] is actually his standard worship word.)

Jesus responds by looking her in the eye and giving voice to the vilest insult that can be made – the insult the other men around the room probably have in their minds, the insult formed from Deuteronomy's picture of the worst of Canaanite idolaters, false worshippers, shrine prostitutes. 'We don't give the children's bread to dogs.' The children – children of Israel, God's beloved. Bread – bread from heaven, manna, God's provision in times of need. Dogs – you. Filthy, immoral, idolatrous, from Deuteronomy 23 to Revelation 22:15 – pagan female you.

And like the tax collector who stands far off, beating his chest and knowing he is a sinner unworthy of forgiveness yet going home cleansed, this woman gets what worship is. She is not an idolater. Her worship is true. 'Sure, I'm far from perfect, not worthy to be here, not on your level, not expecting to sit at the table, not claiming any rights for myself – just hoping for crumbs. Crumbs from you – that's got to be enough. Just the least bit of you, please.' That is right relationship restored. That is the heart of salvation, right there.

I've heard the following false dichotomy raised in the debate about homosexuality in the Church. The stereotype is that liberals say – Come in to all! All are welcome, just as you are! The Church is here for you! But having welcomed all, they kind of leave everyone just as they are, and there is no progress from that moment of welcome. In the same picture, evangelicals look at this and reply – For sure, all are welcome, but all must come

---

36. Greek: *prosekunei*; see Marcus Green, *Salvation's Song*, Survivor Books, 2004, pp.137-40.

ready to change, to know the truth of repentance and the power of God to transform us into the image of Christ. No entrance without repentance.

In the story of the Canaanite woman, for the disciples what was unacceptable about the woman was that she was Canaanite and a woman. I'm pretty sure that after her encounter with Jesus she was still Canaanite and a woman. But she had changed – because her relationship with God had altered fundamentally. She was now a worshipper in spirit and in truth. We are right to seek repentance – but the sin we have to leave behind is not an arbitrarily chosen moral failure. It is our broken relationship with God. That's the fundamental. Repentance is about idolatry first.

When we confuse morality with idolatry we get into a terrible mess. Judgementalism reigns. A straight couple join a church – they look perfect, but secretly it's the most abusive relationship imaginable. Day after day, night after night, the wife totally dominates the husband, destroying him psychologically. Yet at church they are welcomed, they present well, they smile a lot, and soon the wife is on the PCC and everyone loves them. A gay couple want to join the same church but are told from the start that, unless they become celibate, they cannot enter into full fellowship. Nothing else about them – their gifting, their faith, their relationship – matters. What's really needed is for all to experience a deeper transformation of the soul, for all to become deeper worshippers of Jesus. That's the fundamental change, the fundamental repentance, the fundamental call of Romans 12. Our contemporary superficial ecclesiastical stand-offs can simply miss this.

The Opposite of Idolatry

So if my first follow-on from Romans 1 is that gay people are human, what is my second?

Obviously, I do not think the Bible says homosexuality is bad. However, there is a consistent link in the sexuality language of the Scriptures which we cannot ignore, and this consistent link seems to carry a message. Is the message bad news, irrelevant, or spot on?

What's the link I'm talking about?

All the biblical texts we look at find a repeated link between the issue of idolatry and being gay.

It's in every text.

So it's all very well for me to say that the texts aren't about modern sexuality issues – they're about idolatry. But then we are left with a different problem which we have to handle. Is this link a fair observation, is being gay somehow deeply entwined with idolatry – more deeply perhaps than being straight is?

Let's start by accepting the link, and think through what this might mean.

Really bad news

The first option is that this is really bad news.

If it is right to point out some kind of constant link between homosexuality and idolatry in the Scriptures, some might argue that my earlier reference to 'the moral underclass' (judging gay people as in some way 'less' than the rest of humanity) – might actually be an unfair term for a fair response. Being gay could be the cause of a broken relationship with God. Or it might be the result of that broken relationship. Either way, it doesn't really matter. Causally or consequentially, being gay either 'happens' because we are far from God or, having 'happened', it stops us getting close to our Creator. Whichever language we use, heaven actually is padlocked.

So – although I'm trying to persuade you the Bible does not say 'homosexuality: bad news', actually I'm wrong and it really is. Really bad. One way or another, it stops true worship. It makes people less than fully human. It prevents people from becoming fully human.

The problem with this as a reading of the homosexuality/ idolatry link is that, if it is to be seriously considered, it must be considered with all its implications placed front and centre: for if it is true, this actually creates a second-class humanity which receives at most only glancing reference in the Bible. What do I mean, 'a second-class humanity'? I mean a whole subset of people who by their nature cannot reflect God's image as well as the rest of humanity and who are predetermined to live always in a state of broken relationship with God, come what may.

Ultimately unredeemable humanity.

Being gay stops you having a right worshipping relationship.

And if this is the force of the link between homosexuality and idolatry, then why is this nowhere fully explored, and why in Romans when St Paul takes up the reversing of the broken relationship does he not do so pointing out that there are people who by their nature or lifestyle have placed themselves beyond the reach of the gospel love of Christ and cannot benefit? He started with them: why not remind us of the perils they face?

Ultimately unredeemable?

The problem would lie with repentance. Repentance involves a change of mind, a change of heart. I can only speak personally here, for the Scriptures are silent on this, but let me be clear – if I could have changed, over the years I would have become as straight as straight could be. I never chose to be gay; those who know me well know how wilful I can be, but being evangelical and choosing to be gay is beyond even my capacity for orneriness. It's hard to un-choose something you never chose in the first place. And if you can't repent, you can't be redeemed. Sometimes I feel like I'm that Canaanite woman walking into that room of disciples; there's nothing I can do about the very thing that makes you avoid looking at me with those sad eyes of yours. And if a person can't be redeemed then they are in a second class of humanity – about which the Bible is silent. It's not a question of choosing not to have sex, as if that's the answer (put me right, but I don't think straight people only class themselves as straight if they are sexually active, so why reduce homosexual orientation to the sexual act?) – life is about far more than having sex.

And any view that wants to find scriptural pretexts for a permanent or necessary break between gay people and God (creating a biblical basis for a second-class humanity) may well think this link grants it some intellectual credence – but it then has to ignore Jesus. Repeatedly. I went for John 3:17 earlier – but what about John 3:16, anyone? '. . . so that *everyone* who believes in him may not perish but may have eternal life'.

There's no footnote on 'everyone'. It means everyone.

This argument will not do. We need another option.

Really irrelevant

A second basic strand of thought we have to consider, as we think about the linking of idolatry and being gay in the Scriptures, is that it's really just irrelevant.

This is risky. By this strategy, we might render the whole biblical witness simply out of touch with the modern world. Contemporary gay lives do not come within the context of idolatrous pagan worship, which is what the Scriptures apparently discuss. Therefore, the Bible has no contribution to make on the issue for us – beyond, perhaps, reminding us tangentially to value all people, and calling us to fight for justice. That sort of thing. But generally speaking, the Scriptures don't speak to today's questions on homosexuality. For example, as already mentioned – if we ask, should two men fall in love and want to spend their lives together, what is a Christian response? If two women from work are getting married, how do you as a Christian react? The Bible is silent. The question is never asked, never answered. We have to work these things out for ourselves without getting hung up on the centuries-old issues of dark pagan practices that do not apply in the early twenty-first century.

Well, I find interesting things here. Some who hold this view are indeed genuine, passionate evangelicals. But I am the kind of old-school evangelical who is always going to be wary of declaring that any part of the Scriptures does not to speak to us today.

Of course, I fully agree that we must pay proper respect to the call to observe justice for all. That remains especially true for the oppressed and those unable to fight for themselves. Jesus clearly had a very special way of breaking social taboos and spending time with 'sinners' and tax collectors, to the dismay of the Pharisees and of some of his own followers. As we have seen, it can sometimes be slightly lazy theology to think that, for Jesus, time spent with 'sinners' was always time calling them to some form of obvious moral repentance. The Canaanite woman remains Canaanite and a woman. We may not instantly see those categories as 'moral failings', but we aren't first-century Jewish men. Context, context.

Repentance isn't always – or even often – about morality in the Scriptures. It's about life with or without God.

But let's stay with this 'justice' idea for a moment. When Jesus calls Matthew to follow him,[37] Matthew leaves his tax collector's booth and the next thing we know Jesus is having supper at Matthew's house with a whole collection of Matthew's friends – tax collectors like him and other 'sinners'. This can be a confusing scenario for us. Jesus does indeed say he has come to call sinners, and the sick need a doctor – which suggests (if we go back to the false dichotomy I raised a few pages back) that he is here being an evangelical, expecting change. Yet the Pharisees see no transformation in any of the dinner guests; all

---

37. Matthew 9:9-13.

they see is impurity, a rabbi eating with the dross of society – Jesus being the stereotypical liberal in that same picture.

Of course, what Jesus is doing is bringing about a deeper repentance. It's not about morality, it's about dealing with idolatry. It's not about actions, it's about relationship. Mark doesn't call Matthew 'Matthew'; he calls him 'Levi', presumably because of his tribe.[38] And if that's his tribe, it speaks of his calling, his work, his position in society – a role in the families that serve in the Temple in Jerusalem, a role in the leading of the worship of the people of God. But Matthew hasn't been doing this, he has had his back turned on such a gift and a grace, and instead has been earning his living by serving the Roman pagan overlords who are running God's country. A tax collector, a quisling.

Jesus sees this man and bids him be healed. He bids him repent of the brokenness that has led him to turn his back on the worship of his God. Jesus restores Matthew to relationship with his Father God as he begins a relationship with the Son. It's not about morality, it's about sorting out idolatry, broken relationship, lost worship which is the underlying, root, causal, primary sin behind all other things. And the God who loves Matthew loves him completely: so he dwells with him, eats with him, meets with the people who are his life, though that life will indeed never be the same again, as mercy (the gift of love) conquers sacrifice (the demands of law).[39]

This perhaps offers a key for us in answering the idea that idolatry is irrelevant to us today, and we most certainly have to go on to challenge the superficiality of reading the patterns

---

38. Mark 2:14.
39. Matthew 9:13.

of idolatrous worship described in the Scriptures as the only forms of idolatry possible, meant or foreseen. Idolatry is not about pagan temples and wayside gods made out of tree-trunks and metal and gaudily-painted stones: it is about a break in the fundamental relationship between any and every human being and our Creator. It is about a primal relationship of love and worship with God and replacing that love and allowing the eyes of our hearts to be fixed elsewhere. On another person. On another thing. On something else good, perhaps, that we should love – but only One should have the first place in our hearts.

Such a story is never irrelevant.

Really spot on

I think the third way of understanding the problem of the link between being gay and idolatry that pours out of every biblical reference has to be this: for the gay person who would follow Christ, the Scripture clearly has this challenge – have no idols.

Be a worshipper of Jesus.

Tend your heart.

Place Christ in the first place.

Don't be broken; be whole.

I don't think this observation can be avoided, and I don't think a true follower of Jesus would want to avoid it, though it might feel uncomfortable. I certainly don't think straight people should rejoice in the fact that the observation is there and aimed so strongly at gay people (I might take time with texts on adultery and promiscuity otherwise – strangely, given our contemporary stereotypes, the Scriptures aim their warnings here full square and pretty exclusively at heterosexuals) but I do think gay people should face this and embrace it.

The texts that make this link according to this understanding don't say 'homosexuality: bad', but 'homosexuals: beware!' As with other warnings (about lust for example) they do not nullify love, but rather warn against love misplaced. Misused. A bad thing warned against presumes that there can be a good thing to be valued in its place.

In the story of the Rich Young Man in Mark 10:17-31, the young man eagerly tells Jesus of all the commandments he has kept – and reels off commandments five through nine of the Ten. You can almost feel Jesus nodding, urging him to get to number ten. Which he never does. 'Still one to go,' says Jesus, hopefully. Still no response. So the only answer to a blindness on covetousness is to deal with it thoroughly: and Jesus tells the man to let go completely of all those things he is holding on to so firmly. All of them. Everything.

And he can't; the young man goes away, sad.

A bad thing warned against presumes there can be a good thing in its place. Having stuff isn't bad – grasping stuff as though it is the centre of reality, well, that's a different issue. If you want to be able to have, you have to be able to let go. Let it go, says Jesus, for me – put me first, and you'll get back far more than you can imagine. A hundred times. Keep it – and the kingdom of God becomes impossible for you.

Then Jesus flashes his wonderful smile around at his disciples and splashes hope everywhere: 'Impossible for you,' he says, watching the rich young man walking away, and knowing this is not the end of his story, there is more to come, 'but not impossible for God. Onwards and upwards!'

So although idolatry and being gay are linked with a sense of the danger of destruction, yet here constantly is the mercy of God in shining his light on the path that leads to death so that people may walk instead the path that leads to life. The Scriptures do not say that gay people should be straight, or pretend to be so, or hide out of fear; instead, they say: be aware that hearts that will love what is placed before them, and love with passion, must place Jesus in that place. And love him. Passionately. And loving him, love one another.

Romans, again . . .

And we are back in Romans 12 once more . . .

> Let love be genuine; hate what is evil, hold fast to what is good; love one another with mutual affection; outdo one another in showing honour. Do not lag in zeal, be ardent in spirit, serve the Lord. Rejoice in hope, be patient in suffering, persevere in prayer. (Romans 12:9-12)

St Paul reminds us in the opening of Romans 2[40] that the warnings of the first chapter are not just for one class of person; everyone falls on this. He repeats this in the climax of chapter

---

40. Romans 2:1: 'Therefore you have no excuse, whoever you are, when you judge others; for in passing judgement on another you condemn yourself, because you, the judge, are doing the very same things.'

3 (and he's not talking about lying on your tax return: he's got bigger fish to fry), 'since all have sinned and fall short of the glory of God' (Romans 3:23).

We are all of us broken; and all, through Christ, redeemable. The relationship with God can be ours. Ours, everyone's.

In other words – we have no room for a second-class humanity. No room for a moral underclass. It turns out gay people are – people. Subject to the same warnings and encouragements as everybody else. No one is up for special treatment, positively or negatively. Everyone is just as liable to miss the truth and needing just as much to be reminded of God's love; just as loved and just as covered by the Cross which speaks of that love. There is no padlock on heaven's gates. Repentance is possible for all because it brings us all to that place, grateful, open-handed, worshipping in spirit and in truth because of Jesus. Romans 3:23 – none of us can point the finger at anyone else; Romans 3:24 – and all of us receive the same gift of forgiveness and restoration.

We are all human.

One Humanity

Actually, we need to pause and let this thought stay with us for a moment.

I'm going to make a point about Galatians shortly, but there's just a little more life to be drawn from the power of the link between the ideas of sexuality and idolatry before we move on.

We need to understand how encompassing this link is. Very many of the condemnations of idolatry through the Scriptures come in the language of sexual practice. As a metaphor it is strong: what more vivid image is there of faithfulness or its absence? Beyond this, as we have already seen, many of the worship practices of the ancient nations around the Jews historically involved sexual acts. And let's face it, most of the Bible references that pick this up aren't about gays. Far more verses link straight sex and idolatry than idolatry and being gay.

I'll say that last bit again. We've so focused on the link between homosexuality and idolatry that something may just have got missed, and it won't hurt to point it out: far more verses link straight sexual excesses and idolatry than being gay and the same.

Let's just read the Bible.

More than metaphor

For example, take two concepts that are commonplace in Jewish thinking within the Old Testament – two concepts that lie at the heart of Israel's historical abandonment of God: prostitution and adultery. These ideas are actually far more common when it comes to links with idolatry than homosexuality. Far more common. And they are generally put across as heterosexual sins.

Look at Moses' injunction to the people in Exodus 34:15: 'You shall not make a covenant with the inhabitants of the land, for when they prostitute themselves to their gods and sacrifice to their gods, someone among them will invite you, and you will eat of the sacrifice.'

Problem is, we can be so used to reading these Scriptures, and so blind to our own faults, that sometimes really shocking words get allegorised, and plain truth slips into metaphor, so it is more bearable or can be easily applied to a polite middle-class church setting.

It's time to see through the metaphor.

The use of sexual imagery in the Old Testament is not just a picture to shock us into understanding the effects of idolatry ('it's like being so unfaithful to God'). Pagan worship in the ancient world often involved sexual practice. Those Canaanite poems were full of it. After all, there are more straight people around; so as for what mostly went on – work it out. Fertility rites were commonplace,[41] and temples were adorned with sacred pillars. And we're not talking about the Temple in Jerusalem; we're talking about little temples and shrines on hills and under trees, in villages and towns and all over the place. People didn't have to travel to some great religious palace to do this – there was a Tesco Extra on every corner. 'Every little helps.' Let me be blunt: why do people need prostitutes?

Here's the word 'adultery'. Jeremiah 3:6 (NIV): 'During the reign of King Josiah, the Lord said to me, "Have you seen what faithless Israel has done? She has gone up on every high hill and under every spreading tree and has committed adultery there."'

Every high hill, every spreading tree – these are the places where shrines were set up for pagan worship. The 'adultery' practised reflects metaphorically the unfaithfulness of God's people worshipping other things than God; but the metaphor has particular power because of what they'd be physically getting up to in the name of worship. Husbands would forget wives, wives husbands, and the power of worship is always that

---

41. Robert Guisepi, http://history-world.org/canaanite_culture_and_religion.htm

the standards of who or what we worship make us who and what we are. It's actually far more than 'souvenirs'. In the stories, Greek gods cavorted with mortals; so what did the mortals go and do? We copy what we worship; we want to become like whom or what we worship. And actually, that's what happens: we become what we worship.

The Bible story is always that true worship, worship of the One True God, ultimately raises us up; idolatry, worship of any created thing, makes us less.

This is what St Paul is talking about at the start of Romans. In Romans 1, he speaks of the abandonment of true worship of God by using examples of pagan idolatry to make his case, including (but not exclusively) homosexual acts in that context. But then he goes on in Romans 2 (way back I said I'd return to this) to show that the Jews made the same mistakes, and uses adultery (with its overtones of Jeremiah, Ezekiel and the disaster of the Exile) as his example here: 'You that forbid adultery, do you commit adultery? You that abhor idols, do you rob temples? You that boast in the law, do you dishonour God by breaking the law? For, as it is written, "The name of God is blasphemed among the Gentiles because of you"' (Romans 2:22-24).

You think the Gentiles are bad? says St Paul. Look at yourselves! You stick your noses in the air at their idols, and then while you're at it, your backsides too and commit adultery in their temples, breaking faith with the God who loves you, making foreigners spit on his name.

Being human

This isn't a question of gay or straight (issues St Paul never worried about) or even of morality (which he did worry about, but not here) or even ethnicity (which he always worried about, but which he refused to allow to be fundamental, despite the best efforts of all kinds of voices and histories shouting loudly around him) – it's a question of broken or redeemed humanity. The Creator and his relationship with his beloved. It's the Fall, it's the Cross, it's Eden and the wilderness and the long path to a New Heaven and a New Earth.

So yes – the Bible links being gay with idolatry; but (at last, my point!) it also links being straight with idolatry.

The Bible links being human with idolatry.

Indeed, that the Bible links being gay and idolatry, given the rest of its story, is in itself a powerful reminder of how equally human all people are, irrespective of sexual orientation. We are all subject to the same brokenness. And we are all granted the same way out.

The same answer.

The same Saviour.

We are the same.

So (and I said a while back I was going to get here – thanks for waiting) for everyone who believes (and that word 'everyone' really does mean 'everyone'), to all who are 'baptised into Christ', St Paul has important words in Galatians 3:28: 'There is no longer Jew or Greek, there is no longer slave or free, there is no longer male and female; for all of you are one in Christ Jesus.'

CHAPTER THREE

A TRAJECTORY OF HOPE

I hope this hasn't felt too negative ('those texts that you thought meant that, don't'). If there is anything of that in the air, it's time we did something about it. We need a positive theology that embraces the whole swathe of the biblical story to make us forget we ever thought this was all about that teeny-tiny handful of texts we started with.

And saying 'people are people' is all well and good. But every mention of anything to do with homosexuality in the Bible remains inconveniently unfavourable. We remain apparently no closer to any practical answers to the questions we have to face. I've said before that when it comes to the kind of issues that hit us square on ('can it ever be OK if two people of the same gender who are genuinely Christian, trying to be genuinely godly, find themselves in a faithful and loving relationship and want to commit to each other for life – and for that relationship to be sexual?') there are surely days when the most inclusive Bible teacher has to shrug their shoulders: as far as the Bible goes, in those terms the questions are never asked, never answered.

Is that all there is – on the traditionalist side, proof texts that don't say what they seem to; on the revisionist side, silence and a shrug?

One other thing I've already said is that, when evangelicals struggle to understand something, we use the Scripture to interpret the Scripture. The Bible is brilliant at giving us principles that unlock the truth. That's where we are here; it's not 'silence and a shrug' – and it's not being satisfied by proof texts either. Neither of these are sufficient for us. We need more.

There is more.

Neither slave nor free

'Neither slave nor free' (Galatians 3:28). It has become a commonplace to liken the change in attitude we seek over homosexuality to the change that was once wrought in the hearts and minds of nations over slavery. Once, the Church and the wider world both saw texts in the Bible that actually approved of slavery. Then people realised there was a bigger picture. Eyes were opened. Hearts were changed.

So, the argument goes, with homosexuality.

I have seen this put across in different ways. One excellent evangelical scholar, for whom I have the deepest respect,[42] dismisses this comparison on the grounds that he finds a redemptive trajectory on the story of slavery within the Scriptures themselves which points towards the eventual position we now hold. For sure, he says, the Bible always had room for the dignity of the slave, but through time and into the writings of the New Testament, there was the development of hope which paved the way for the abolitionist movements of the eighteenth and nineteenth centuries.

---

42. Tim Tennent, http://seedbed.com/feed/slaves-women-and-homosexuals February 2013.

He finds no such redemptive trajectory for gay people to cling to.

Well, I am afraid that I am one of those awkward people who is never quite as convinced by that trajectory away from slavery within the Scriptures. I apologise for this. For me, the Scriptures exist with a continuous and difficult tension: the equality of persons created in the image of God is clear. But so too is the fallenness of society and the way people are used within the societies of Bible times. The role of God's people is to raise others up – so slavery in the Old Testament has safeguards on it. Slavery may happen, it does happen, but it may never be absolute. There are jubilees (Leviticus 25:39-43), proclamations of release (Deuteronomy 15:12-18), decrees of hope, and at the beginning the fourth commandment of the Ten in Exodus 20 insists that the Sabbath is to include the maidservant and manservant. Exodus 23 specifically includes in that commandment 'the slave born in your house' (NIV) or 'your home-born slave' (NRSV).

This isn't a story of development. This is a tale of safeguards and indicators placed on a fallen humanity from the very beginning. This is why those who opposed the ending of slavery in Britain and the US and elsewhere were wrong but not – in their day – ridiculous. We are too quick to judge others by the standards of our own time; this is neither historically nor biblically fair.

Experience of hope

In the New Testament, Paul's plea about Onesimus ('have him back for ever, no longer as a slave but as more than a slave, a beloved brother' (Philemon:15-16)) does not simply reject slavery in the new light of the freedom Christ brings, but offers a way of living that is true to all that the Scripture already demonstrates. It's not new, it's authentic. The slave/master exhortations of, say, Ephesians 6 also come within this framework. There is no sudden change, no trajectory toward change, even. All live in the brokenness. Those who (hundreds of years later) came to argue that abolition had to be better, that freedom was more godly, that equality more reflected how people truly are had to do so by claiming higher truths than a mere battle of proof texts could allow. Arguing for the status quo and against change wasn't hard; Wilberforce in Britain and Lincoln in the US had to use other biblical places than texts on slavery in order to make their case.

Richard Burridge of King's College, London, argues that it wasn't simply the biblical story that changed the slavery debate.[43] He gives the biblical arguments used by both sides and then looks at the impact that Wilberforce, Granville Sharp, the Clarkson brothers and the Clapham sect made by revealing the realities of the contemporary slave trade to the British public. They told stories. They publicised facts. They made the truth personal, and they made it known. Josiah Wedgwood designed a medallion inscribed with the slogan 'Am I not a man and a brother?' over a picture of a slave. Olaudah Equiano was a slave from Ghana; he was freed and very successfully published his story in 1789. John Newton's great contribution came around the same time with the publication of his work, *Thoughts upon the African Slave Trade*, nearly forty years after

---

43. The Revd Dr Richard Burridge, 'Slavery, Sexuality and the Inclusive Community', 22nd Eric Symes Abbott Memorial Lecture, 2007.

his conversion. Burridge comments: 'If there was biblical study driving the abolitionists, it was a result of reading and re-reading their Bibles in the light of that listening to the experience of former slaves and slave-traders.'

Matthew Vines, writing in his book *God and the Gay Christian*, is careful to comment: 'Neither Peter in his work to include Gentiles in the church nor the abolitionists in their campaign against slavery argued that their experience should take precedence over Scripture. But they both made the case that their experience should cause Christians to reconsider long-held interpretations of Scripture.'[44]

Treasured texts were shaped by real voices. And people heard the word.

The same story, heard differently

So in line with Vines and Burridge and against Tim Tennent (whom I repeat I admire enormously), I actually do think it may be possible to argue for a 'trajectory of redemption' on the homosexuality question within the scriptural witness. It may be the stories of real people we meet that open our ears, but then with newly opened ears we hear the Bible freshly. The Bible itself starts to rewrite the story of how gay people are seen. And I think it is some of the very texts that are often used to argue against the acceptance of homosexuality that take us there.

Leviticus 20:13 enforces the death penalty on practising homosexuals: 'If a man lies with a male as with a woman, both of them have committed an abomination; they shall be put to death; their blood is upon them.'

---

44. Vines, *God and the Gay Christian*, p.15.

There is, however, no question of the death penalty for homosexuality in the New Testament. That's a change.

I mean – that's a huge change.

It's a huge change because of what it represents in terms of attitudes to sexuality, and more, because these texts aren't primarily about sexuality anyway. Sex in Leviticus was about idolatry; Paul talks in the same terms in the New Testament – he's not writing about sex *per se*, but about human behaviour that comes as evidence of idolatry.

So what's the difference? Where's the evidence for this 'trajectory of hope'?

The evidence is simple and clear. The place that comes closest to offering the language of Leviticus 20 in the New Testament is Romans 1:32. It says that there are people who 'deserve to die' because of their actions. What actions? Well, they include a very long list in Romans 1:28-31 – for example, gossiping and disobeying parents. Homosexual acts back in Romans 1:27 were not deemed capital offences; people merely 'received in their own persons the due penalty for their error'. Even the most traditionalist reading of this has to say – there's been some softening from the Levitical bloodlust.

But much more than that: we have already seen how Romans 1 and Romans 2 belong together. Paul attacks the sin of the world – idolatry, the end of right relationship with God, the loss of righteousness, the victory of sin (which a former Welsh churchwarden of mine wonderfully entitles 'wrong-shusness') –

and brings into play his stereotypes whereby for the Gentile that looks like perversion, and for the Jew it looks like prostitution. He then goes on to say: 'There will be anguish and distress for everyone who does evil, the Jew first and also the Greek, but glory and honour and peace for everyone who does good, the Jew first and also the Greek' (Romans 2:9-10).

This is the huge change.

In Leviticus, an act had a consequence. The consequence was simply death. One act, one result. Committing the act in the first place was seen as the result of abandoning God, seen by some as the definition of abandoning God, certainly as the caricature of what pagans who did not know God got up to – so the Act was by definition Deathly.

Now, St Paul uses that act as an example of how those who have abandoned God can return and know eternal life. There is hope. And this includes Jews and Gentiles. Idolaters all. There is hope for everyone.

Because it wasn't just the perverse pagan who was an idolater, was it? It was the self-righteous Jew too. The Exile, the great disaster that threw God's people out of God's land, didn't happen as a result of what the Gentiles did. It happened because of the unfaithfulness of God's own people. Their adultery, metaphorical and literal.

So when the Cross opens the door to redemption, it flings it wide open to everyone. And Paul expresses this by using shockingly vivid language.

This is absolutely the trajectory of hope, the story of redemption, and it includes those whose brokenness from

God is typified by whatever kind of moral failing, whether they be Gentile or Jew. The New Covenant really is New. Romans, perhaps the New Testament text that has been used above all others to say homosexuality is bad and forbidden and beyond the pale, in fact finds itself to be the very text that brings all sorts of people into the realm of redemption: 'since all have sinned and fall short of the glory of God; they are now justified by his grace as a gift, through the redemption that is in Christ Jesus' (Romans 3: 23-24).

Throw away the padlock, and be done with the moral underclass. People are people. There is neither Gentile nor Jew. Neither Romans 1 offender, nor Romans 2 offender. Not in spite of St Paul, but because of him. This is some arc of hope right here.

Let's push this further. Paul is talking about those whose brokenness from God has made them moral offenders – adulterers and prostitutes and homosexual offenders. But does he mean to say all gay people are homosexual offenders? Is he saying that all straight people are adulterers?

Or might we see that if hope exists for such as these, perhaps we might find it too for those who are not 'offenders'. Those who are decent but different.

If only the text gave us such an example.

Oh – wait a moment, it does!

Building the story of hope

Again, I will repeat with apologies that I don't see the clear redemptive trajectory in the Bible story concerning slavery.

Moses recognises slavery and also recognises it is imperfect. He ensures room for redemption from the beginning, and presses for good care of slaves. When it comes to slavery, Paul lives in Moses' world. The same place. Room for room.

But already, in Chapter One of this book, we have seen that Moses' world was abandoned in the New Testament when it came to – for example – eunuchs.

Eunuchs. Not people we often think about. Not people regarded normally as 'offenders'. Not rapists. Might these be those 'decent but different' people we can read of in the biblical text?

Let's look at how hope takes hold of their story through the pages of the Scriptures.

Back at the beginning of Chapter One, I referred to Deuteronomy 23:1 and recommended the Authorised Version for the full effect: 'He that is wounded in the stones, or hath his privy member cut off, shall not enter into the congregation of the Lord.'

Nice.

Eunuchs are forbidden from entering the congregation of the faithful; their sexual ambivalence was not acceptable. Moses is clear.

But this changes – even within the Old Testament.

In Isaiah (several hundred years after Moses) a time is prophesied when they will be welcome in the Temple, the presence of God: 'do not let the eunuch say, 'I am just a dry tree.' For thus says the

Lord: To the eunuchs who keep my sabbaths, who choose the things that please me and hold fast my covenant, I will give, in my house and within my walls, a monument and a name better than sons and daughters; I will give them an everlasting name that shall not be cut off' (Isaiah 56:3-5).

If there is any question of their physicality or sexuality being linked with idolatry in Moses, Isaiah sweeps that to one side. Eunuchs might be eunuchs, and yet might also be godly – keepers of the covenant. Their reward? 'An everlasting name' in the Temple. In the Temple. In God's very presence.

Coming into the New Testament period, Jesus, in Matthew 19:12, makes their state no mere mistake, but even a sign of grace and godliness: 'For there are eunuchs who have been so from birth, and there are eunuchs who have been made eunuchs by men, and there are eunuchs who have made themselves eunuchs for the sake of the kingdom of heaven' (ESV).

Some use this reference to be an encouragement to celibacy; Jesus and Paul both knew the word for celibacy, and Paul uses it, but Jesus here does not. He chooses not to. Folk argue over what 'eunuchs for the sake of the kingdom of heaven' might mean, but what it doesn't mean is Deuteronomy 23. Jesus now accords people once given no option but death a place in his Book of Life.

And this story arc reaches completion in Acts 8:26-39 with the conversion and baptism of the Ethiopian eunuch by Philip. It's no coincidence it's Isaiah he reads; and it's Life he receives. He confesses Jesus, is baptised, and onward the eunuch goes, rejoicing. Still a eunuch, but in right relationship with his Saviour. That's what I mean by a biblical trajectory of hope, a story of redemption. That's some journey from Deuteronomy right there. From exclusion to family. From exile to home.

Here is a welcoming of those whom God's people had formerly cast out. Decent but different, the eunuch is not a rapist or a sexual offender. He can't repent of being a eunuch. I would not be surprised if Philip took some stick for what he did from those who wanted a strict keeping of Moses' rules. But Luke records it as grace, as holiness, as wonder and as right. 'What is to prevent me from being baptized?' (Acts 8:36). Well – in days gone by, quite a lot; but now – nothing. Nothing at all. A eunuch, a sexually ambiguous foreigner, becomes a member of Christ's church.

The culture of hope

You see, I hate all that 'you're just finding ways to explain away what was said' stuff. I have no intention of explaining anything *away*. To understand what the Bible is actually saying sometimes we have to understand more than the surface. We have to work to get results.

It's worth the work.

The thing is, cultural questions don't only come from the first century. Sometimes we have to recognise that we are more affected than we think by ways of seeing things that are given to us within our own setting in our own time.

I remember the first time I lived abroad. It was early 1990 and I was fortunate to be travelling around the US. Sunday by Sunday I visited church after church, and whilst the people I met were lovely, honest, genuine Christian folk who loved worshipping God, I was struggling. I'd go to church service after church service and find myself bemused. No matter how hard I looked, I couldn't find Jesus anywhere in what was going on.

The fault, of course, was not with the churches I visited – it was with me. Week by week I was dismayed by how the worship in all these churches I went to was just so ... American. And then eventually it hit me. There was a reason for this.

We were in America.

As I worshipped in a different culture I suddenly became aware how culture-bound my own experiences and expectations of God were. And I became very grateful that God meets us where we are, and speaks to us in languages we understand.

Culture, the way we work and think and view the world, is a language.

We have a common cultural background which includes the fact that, when I was born, homosexual acts between consenting adults were illegal. For many people older than me, this was taken as a simple reflection of biblical morality; it was 'normal' and was never thought about beyond that. The implications that this 'biblical morality' had on the lives of thousands of people were not considered. The suicide of a man like Alan Turing went unnoticed and disregarded by most. So much for compassion. So much for loving your neighbour, or your enemy, or anyone else Jesus might have meant us to love.

For me it is not the cultural background noise of the first century but this twentieth-century cultural noise which creates so much of our contemporary theological havoc.

An example of this is how St Paul's words in 1 Corinthians 6 are linked with Leviticus 20 in our theological debates. Technical descriptions are given of the sexual terms used.[45] It's said that the Greek Septuagint version of the Old Testament uses the same words[46] as St Paul. The argument is made that what Leviticus forbids, the New Testament forbids. Simple: gay is bad.

Well – that link can only be made if there is a pre-fixed setting in our understanding which somehow filters out the kind of biblical context work we as evangelicals should do on this and any other issue. It only works if there is no trajectory of hope, and it only works if 1 Corinthians 5 and 6 actually say: 'Now, about what those gay people get up to: this is how you should respond.'

1 Corinthians 6: The End of Hope?

So let's look at this bit of St Paul now. I'm going to do my best to try to pull a little cultural wool from our eyes, though as always when looking at texts and drawing out differing interpretations, I'd invite everyone to read serious alternative views as well. This book is called *The Possibility of Difference*, not *The Insistence You Join My Gang* – because firstly I think we can have a different biblical understanding of sexuality as evangelicals, and secondly we should always, always be able to discuss the Bible freely with open hearts and honest goodwill. When we disagree, we smile, we pray, we love, we live on together.

---

45. Sam Allberry's article 'What does the Bible say about homosexuality?' on the Living Out website is a good example of a traditionalist line here, and indeed on several texts: www.livingout.org/the-bible-and-ssa
46. *malakoi* and *arsenokoitai*.

So here goes:

> Do you not know that wrongdoers will not
> inherit the kingdom of God? Do not be deceived:
> Neither the sexually immoral nor idolaters nor
> adulterers nor men who have sex with men
> nor thieves nor the greedy nor drunkards nor
> slanderers nor swindlers will inherit the kingdom
> of God. And that is what some of you were.
> (1 Corinthians 6:9-11, NIV)

In a moment I want to pull the text apart and see what's really going on. Before I do, I have to stop for a moment and pull the translation apart.

I'm quoting the NIV for a reason here. There is a problem. The NIV used to translate the Greek words *malakoi* and *arsenokoitai* as 'male prostitutes' and 'homosexual offenders'. It now offers 'men who have sex with men' to cover both. This is exactly what I mean about our contemporary culture affecting our understanding of Scripture.

There's a general problem with understanding the Greek. Different people offer slightly different technical translations of exactly what these terms mean. All translations reflect this. The NRSV, for example, goes with 'prostitutes' and 'sodomites'. I'm not an expert on linguistics, but I know this: the impact of saying 'sex worker and predator' is very different from saying 'person who is sexually active'. The NIV used to go for the former; now it chooses the latter.

In our culture, with our conflict over the place of homosexuality in life and in the Church, this is a very active theological choice. It's a very active choice because the text in 1 Corinthians 6:11 goes on to say: 'And that is what some of you were. But you were washed, you were sanctified, you were justified in the name of the Lord Jesus Christ and by the Spirit of our God.'

Do you see? 'You used to be a sex worker and predator – but you were washed, sanctified and justified' is a very long way from saying 'You used to be in an active gay relationship – but you were washed, sanctified and justified, so you can't be any more.'

Not all gays are prostitutes and predators. Not even the sexually active ones. Sorry if that comes as a surprise. Even Hillary Clinton, in her famous gaffe from the 2016 US presidential race thought that only half of Donald Trump's supporters belonged to the 'basket of deplorables'. And then apologised for saying 'half' . . . So again, I want to offer the concept of 'decent but different' as something of a corrective for the mis-labelling of all gay people as rapists. The NIV translators have made a remarkable choice here that seems to have an awful lot more to do with the times we live in than the text in front of them. Perhaps they should carry on in the same manner! Following on from 'men who have sex with men', the list in 1 Corinthians 6:10 might read: 'neither people who use Amazon, nor those who watch *Bake Off*, nor women who like white wine, nor celebrities who comment on Twitter, nor contestants on *The Apprentice* will inherit the kingdom of God. And that's what some of you were, but thank God we're better than that now.'

Hoping for understanding

'Men who have sex with men.' What if that line was 'men who go around having sex with women'? Then would it be promiscuity being attacked, or would it be heterosexuality? The NIV translation as it stands might mean promiscuity, it might mean anything. It isn't a translation – it's a theological choice. It's shocking, but it's a terrific example of how our culture makes us make choices – and sometimes we aren't even aware we're doing it.

As I've said before – I think a lot of the hurtful things that get said in this debate get said wholly without intention of offence. And just occasionally, I wonder . . .

But let's do better. Let's look properly at this text. In fact, before reading on, stop for a moment, pick up your Bible and read the whole of 1 Corinthians 5. Read it again.

I hope you have noticed that most of the passage we are looking at from 1 Corinthians 6 occurs almost word for word twice in 1 Corinthians 5 as well. I hope you have noticed we aren't in the middle of a simple explanation of Christian attitudes to homosexuality. (There's no text saying 'What you should think about those gays . . .' anywhere to be found.) Rather, Paul is calling for purity across the fellowship, for faith to mean something in the lives of all believers, for truth to be lived out consistently. 1 Corinthians 5 starts with the horror of excesses not even pagans get up to (he's referring to the perils of a twisting of heterosexual marriage). There's a call for the yeast that works through the whole batch to be sincerity and truth. And then he says (1 Corinthians 5:9-10) to avoid the immoral, the greedy, the swindler, the idolater. He doesn't mean non-believers, those beyond the fellowship – that would mean leaving the world. Well, it would mean leaving Corinth! No. He makes it clear: someone inside the fellowship (and here's the first repeat) shouldn't be (1 Corinthians 5:11) sexually immoral, greedy, an idolater, a slanderer or a swindler.

A Christian shouldn't live like a pagan Gentile.

You're a Christ follower now. A true worshipper of God. Righteous – right with God.

Then Paul is taken up by the idea that, in disputes, members of the fellowship take their problems back to those outside – to the ungodly, the Gentile – for judgement. Having the dispute is failure enough. Taking it to the pagan unbeliever is failure upon failure. Why? Because how can unbelievers know God's mind? His kingdom doesn't belong to (second repeat, 1 Corinthians 6:9-10) the sexually immoral, idolaters, adulterers, gay prostitutes and predators, thieves, the greedy, drunkards, slanderers or swindlers. It doesn't belong to desperately pagan Gentile idolaters – to the world the Corinthian faithful used to belong to.

Desperately pagan, gloriously redeemed

I'm taking my time here, because taking time is what we need to do with these texts. Paul is describing a world where Christians are those who have been restored to a right relationship with God, which fundamentally is about right worship. Worship that makes sense, to use his phrase from Romans 12. Worship that transforms our understanding and therefore reshapes and restores the way we live our lives. It's a million miles from the idolatry of the forum and the back street, from the orgies of pagan temples, from the loss of identity that comes from worshipping a created thing rather than the Creator.

That's Paul's picture. He uses his usual worldview, his usual caricatures, his usual hyperbole to remind them: Christians are called to a higher standard than those around them. People are not throw-away consumables. That much is entirely consistent with Leviticus. But Paul doesn't call for death penalties; this is the redemptive trajectory at work. He calls for change and for hope and for discipline and for fellowship and for a way of life that is so attractive it changes the world around it. That is a world away from Leviticus. Paul builds this slowly and carefully, repeat upon repeat, phrase upon phrase.

And if the 'Apostle to the Gentiles' doesn't seem to have a very high opinion of those Gentiles (swindlers, slanderers, greedy, immoral, thieves, drunkards, gay prostitutes and predators) yet he works with them, because those things aren't the core of the problem.

No.

Paul is consistent as the day. We are back to Romans 1.

The sin of the world is nothing to do with homosexuality or heterosexuality or women who drink too much white wine or any moral deal at all. Romans 1 is clear: the sin of the world is idolatry. 'They exchanged the truth about God for a lie and worshipped and served the creature rather than the Creator, who is blessed for ever!' (Romans 1:25). That's the heart of the problem. Everything comes from here.

In Jesus' words – what is the greatest commandment? To love God.

So in Paul's words – what is the greatest sin? To love something or someone in God's place. Idolatry.

Back to the trajectory of hope, the story of redemption. Amazingly, here's the real change. If there was any hope in Leviticus, it was for the Jew. The festivals of forgiveness dotted through that book painted a picture of a possibility of change for God's chosen race. Now, in 1 Corinthians for Paul it's for the Gentile too.[47] For everyone.

People are people.

The Scripture has changed the pitch. In Leviticus, two men lying together were a sign of idolatry, being like pagans, abandoning God and being worthy of the death penalty. In Paul, certain homosexual acts (that's the clearest we can get; we don't really know what kind of acts, and he says nothing at all of relationships) are equated with idolatry but so is virtually everything else (from greed to gossip to slander to adultery, moral sins which are not respecters of sexual orientation) and it is the linking of all these moral failures with the greater sin of idolatry that really exercises Paul – and yet still Jesus is there for all.

For all. Offering hope. Redemption. Life, not death.

Questions of hope

Now: here's the question that the Church has to face up to today; the question that the Bible doesn't ask directly and therefore gives no direct answer to, but which these passages from 1 Corinthians frame for us rather well.

---

47. See, for example, 1 Corinthians 1:23-24.

What happens when my heart belongs to Jesus, when I worship him in Spirit and truth, genuinely, and have therefore put aside idolatry and with it immorality, swindling, gossiping (even), disobeying my parents (let's just imagine), but find I still love deeply someone else of the same gender and want to commit to being with them? Do the moral details of Romans 1 or Romans 2 or the prostitutes and predators of 1 Corinthians 6 speak to my situation any more than Leviticus 20?

In short: are the acts of idolatry the only acts possible for gay people? Is the choice between idolatry and abstinence the Bible's only story?

Or does the trajectory of hope, the observed movement towards redemption within the Scriptures, the change from death penalty to salvation, the baptising of the decent but different eunuch even, point to a possibility not explicitly stated? If there is the hope that the stereotypical Gentile losing herself in sex with another woman during acts of idolatrous worship might be saved; if there's the same salvation hope for the stereotypical Jew losing himself in sex with a prostitute, committing adultery literally and spiritually as he worships away from home; if there's hope for the decent but different eunuch to be made a member of God's family and to worship with the company of the believing faithful, Jew and Gentile – how much more hope is there?

This is the territory where our contemporary questions begin to touch the ground of biblical argument.

Let's go back to the slavery comparison for a moment, and to an example we again mentioned earlier. One of the kindest master/slave relationships in the Bible, of course, lies outside the people of God. The centurion who loved his slave and comes to Jesus in Matthew 8:5-13 crosses cultural, social and religious bounds to beg for his slave's life. How lucky that slave was to have such a master! And we honour that master – and we honour Jesus, for restoring to life someone who may have been at heaven's door, and instead resumes a life of being a chattel, a thing (however prized). Less than a person. Legally a belonging. Oh, the redemptive story of slavery through the Scriptures.

Now let's look at that story through a different lens.

We've been here before. Remember? Luke[48] calls the slave a 'doulos', a slave. Matthew calls him a 'pais', a boy. Matthew's word is sometimes used of the junior partner in a gay relationship in the military – a hierarchical relationship, but not necessarily an abusive one as we might suppose in our culture. Again, we need to make sure our cultural references aren't tainting our view; it was a hierarchical relationship but not a hidden one. Was it perfect? Who knows? But the depth of feelings involved caused an army officer to risk reputation and standing by begging a religious leader from an oppressed nation to help. Is it possible? Is it thinkable that Jesus restores not a 'thing' to be used, but a person to be loved?

Please – listen very carefully to the point I'm making here. Because I'm not asking that this gay-friendly interpretation of Matthew 8 be exclusively upheld. I don't for a moment happen to agree with those (from Gerd Theissen onwards) who argue for it being the only way to read these words. I'm an evangelical. There just isn't enough in the Scripture to make this the necessary way to go. At best, it's a grace-note, a hint, a nod towards a possibility.

---

48. Luke 7:1-10.

My point is this: what is our emotional, gut response to that possibility?

That we'd rather the boy had been a slave than gay?

Because if for a moment as we look at that passage that is our emotional response, then we have discovered an enormous amount about ourselves, and how we react to the whole concept of 'trajectory of hope'. And we've fairly located where the cultural baggage really is.

The implications of hope

The issue is clear, and it is momentous. This is why it is a key argument for those who would not find positive attitudes towards gays within the Scriptures and for those who would. The moment there is a possibility of this arc of hope, of the love of Christ having biblical precedent for the gay person as well as for everyone else, then the end of the story is already written.

That's a big deal, whichever side of the issue you take.

It's not about wanting to 'win' or 'be on the right side of history', but about grasping the compelling nature of the Scriptures that drive us to understand how God in Christ loves and redeems and welcomes each and every person. The end of the story was written before the creation of the world, and the trajectory of hope, the story of redemption God grants us is glorious and on every page of his word. That redemption is for Jew and Gentile, slave and free, male and female – straight and gay.

Jesus welcomes the woman at the well, the Canaanite woman with the sick daughter, Zacchaeus the quisling tax collector, the centurion with the fondness for his slave, the bandit on the next cross – and he welcomes them because they are people. Human beings. There are no social, political, cultural, gender or religious barriers that keep us from him or make us a second-tier moral underclass in his sight.

This is the beginning of our positive theology. This is how we move away from simply arguing against how certain proof texts have denied certain people certain rights. This is how we begin to proclaim the greater message of freedom.

But straight and gay isn't in Paul's list in Galatians 3:28!

Some will argue that the simple reason orientation isn't addressed in Galatians (or anywhere else in Paul) is that orientation is itself a modern concept. The concept of 'being' homosexual was unknown until not much over one hundred years ago. People 'did' homosexual acts; there was no question of 'being gay'. The biblical references are therefore all to doing, not to being. The way we look at the world has changed – and that's part of the work we are having to do today.

This is in part why the 'love the sinner, hate the sin' line comes into play. Many people recognise it is the acts that are spoken of on the page, not the orientation. The orientation is not condemned; the acts are, they say. So this line is used with kind intent because there is ultimately no difficulty with a single, celibate rector of a traditionalist church in a university town.

But it will not do.

Jesus never said, 'Love the sinner, hate the sin.' As Bishop John Pritchard said at his farewell service in Christ Church Cathedral, Oxford, 'Jesus said love God, love your neighbour, and while you're at it, love your enemy too. Any questions?' [49]

If we separate too much what is going on inside a person from what is going on outside, we are in danger of loving a false image of our neighbour, a false image of our enemy, and not of loving the person God loves at all. Time and again Jesus makes it clear that our lives reveal our hearts. They do so because they must. We cannot help it, we are made this way, as complete beings. A good tree bears good fruit – it must. A bad tree bears bad fruit – it can't help it.[50] If our hearts are far from God, then out of our hearts and our mouths come all kinds of evil deeds.[51] And if we have been forgiven much, we will love much in return.[52] Truth will out.

And if there is good fruit, then we should be careful what we call bad.

Look, I would hope all of us might see the problems in any sexual acts that come from us losing ourselves in the worship of world, self, another, power, gain, greed or anything that breaks the true humanity found in the worship of the One True God. And I want to join the dots that Paul joins and grab the force of his argument about the power of idolatry ruining lives in too, too many ways. But when the Bible says 'no longer Jew or Greek', part of that has to mean no barrier of prejudice between people who find themselves with different sexual orientations, because all need Christ.

---

49. Christ Church, Oxford, 30 October 2014.
50. Matthew 7:18.
51. Matthew 15:7-20.
52. Luke 7:47.

Am I arguing no one is sinful? Is that part of my vision of equal humanity? Well, saying we are all equally human is the foundation of a biblical theology for the acceptance of gay people, but this is a million miles from saying 'There are no sinners.' That would be ridiculous, and it would make a nonsense of a gospel of grace. But it also makes a nonsense of a gospel of grace to say St Paul's demolition of barriers works for everyone except gay people, because they are so intrinsically sinful – when the Bible does not make this point. Think about the logic for a moment: so there's no Greek or Jew, a fundamental barrier almost from page one of the Bible, but yes, there is still straight or gay, which God almost forgot to mention? Really? Of course, there are some sinful gay people whose orientation makes life worse for them; and exactly the same goes for some sinful straight people. And, for all, there is Jesus. He is the only universal answer.

To impose celibacy (as some of my dearest evangelical friends argue) on an entire swathe of humanity, as if it were possible (and as if it were being kind) as a one-size-fits-all-solution, takes us back to an unintended ethical black hole, and to the moral underclass, not to the Cross. We may not have meant to go there, but . . . Let's not go where we didn't mean to; let us always follow the way of the Cross.

People are people. Made in God's image. Re-makeable in that image. Remarkable in that image. Implausibly different from one another; and whether all those differences will be celebrated or even noticed in heaven, for now it ought to be the glory of that image, not the smallness of our grasp upon it, that makes the wonder of his love and his word shine through by the power of his Spirit.

But Galatians 3:28 Isn't About Sin!

If you've wanted to shout this sentence at me for the last few pages, I apologise.

I want to take this objection seriously and look at it full in the face. There are many people for whom this is a serious matter of biblical interpretation, and there are many others who get this serious matter of biblical interpretation thrown in their faces. We need to be able to understand the objection and understand how we might answer it.

Here's the objection: it's all very nice to say there's one humanity, that all people are equal, that we're all the same – but if one's basic understanding of homosexuality is that it is portrayed in the Scriptures as intrinsically sinful, what then? St Paul doesn't make grace and sin equal things. Quite the opposite! So people who resolutely refuse to live by God's standards are not equal to those who repent and live under grace.

Evangelicals who agree and disagree about this objection will have a lot in common. Let's keep to our understanding of Galatians 3:28.

No longer Jew or Greek – OK, so there had to be an ethnic shift in the thinking of some early Christians that God's plans were bigger than they thought. But these folk were just different races; they were still people. We are all clear on this.

No male or female – OK, so women and men together receive God's promises; it's not like you can repent and stop being a woman. The Scriptures don't make being female sinful. They do make certain attitudes to women unacceptable, attitudes which have to be lost as everyone is equally made in God's image, and equally redeemed. We're pretty fine with this, mostly, though a lot of women have had to endure a lot of fighting to get us to this place. I said before, Reformation 500 year saw the #MeToo Movement and all their work recognised as *Time Magazine*'s person of the year. About time too.

No slave or free – OK, so society (and this includes the Church) has historically treated people with different values, but the Scriptures make clear that people are people and have ultimate equal worth even if from time to time that has got lost. The Church is the place where this worth should be found again, even if back in the home or the market place or the street, true reality is removed once more. Slavery is a superficial deceit of this world. People are people.

But gay and straight? This is where we struggle. For many traditionalists, these are not equivalent categories to the ones above, because they are not about the colour of a person's skin or about natural gender or about economic happenstance. Gay and straight are about sin. Straight is 'natural' and therefore godly. Gay is 'unnatural' and therefore ungodly. Period. And try as I might to argue for inclusivity, there is always a difficulty for some (even if many of us argue it is based on the supremacy of a teeny-tiny number of texts over the vast majority of scriptural sense) in allowing such a concept of inclusivity because it seems to mean ignoring *sin*.

Being clear about sin

May I be clear? I do not ignore sin.

But may I also gently suggest that all of us need to be very clear indeed what is sin, and what sin is, before we kindly continue to condemn our own brothers and sisters to the purgatory that the spirit of previous ages placed upon them.

In answering the objection raised here, I find the Jew/ Greek question in Galatians 3:28 very helpful. We need to get to grips with this question of sin and how much it defines the gay/straight dichotomy. And as we look at that, let's also take a brief look at that natural/unnatural antithesis that gets bandied about from Romans 1.

Gentile sinners

The first thing to note is that in the Scriptures the Jew/Greek distinction is never simply ethnic. Actually, that's an ironic choice of words. The Greek here for 'Greek' is 'ethnes', from which we derive words like ethnic. It means 'nations' or 'clans'. People groups. Perhaps I might better express myself by saying that the Jew/Greek distinction isn't simply racial. The choice of the word 'Greek' as a translation can be confusing – it doesn't mean people from Greece! The NIV tends to go for the wider 'Gentiles'; the NRSV uses both 'Greek' and 'Gentile'. It's the same word in the original, whichever English word we find in translation.

Paul explains more of the Jew/Greek distinction in Galatians 2:15-16: 'We ourselves are Jews by birth and not Gentile sinners; yet we know that a person is justified not by the works of the law but through faith in Jesus Christ.' 'Gentile sinners . . .' Those who aren't Jews 'by birth' are actually, it seems, a particular kind of intrinsically sinful person.

By nature.

Why? How?

The nations, the clans, the Gentiles are 'sinners' because they don't have God. They don't have his Law, his prophets, his story, they are not his people. The relationship is broken; they live in 'wrong-shusness' not righteousness. They have other gods. They are idolaters. It's not a moral statement. It's fundamentally spiritual. Sin in St Paul always is – and not only in St Paul.

Here's a helpful command from Leviticus, with God speaking to his people: 'You shall be holy to me; for I the Lord am holy, and I have separated you from the other peoples to be mine' (Leviticus 20:26).

All the moral imperatives that we fixate on in the Old Testament Law are secondary to the religious commands. They cannot be understood without being seen from that spiritual perspective. When looking at the Old Testament Law, always ask – what does this reveal about the character of God? What does this reveal about the contrasting character of the religious understanding of Israel's neighbours?

'You must not do as they do in Egypt, where you used to live, and you must not do as they do in the land of Canaan, where I am bringing you. Do not follow their practices. You must obey my laws and be careful to follow my decrees. I am the Lord your God' (Leviticus 18:3-4, NIV).

Don't be like them, don't take on their standards, don't live in the light of their worship and what that means for their lives. Live like you belong to me! That's God's message to his children: relationship is all.

So the division between Jews and Gentiles isn't racial – where you are born or the colour of your skin. It isn't about morality – how you view right and wrong. It's rather about the very heart of sin. On the one hand we have a nation who follow the

Lord with all their heart, and on the other all the other nations of the world who exhibit with every breath the very broken relationship between creature and Creator, loving first anything and everything other than the One who loves them. One nation and one nation only lives in right relationship with God; every other lives at best in ignorance, and always in brokenness.

This is the sin of the Gentiles. Romans 1. Broken relationship with God. Idolatry.

And yet in Christ, says St Paul, this is swept away.

What is the result of the saving work of Christ upon the sin of the Gentiles?

'That the Gentiles might glorify God for his mercy' (Romans 15:9).
'Rejoice, O Gentiles, with his people!' (Romans 15:10).
'In him the Gentiles shall hope' (Romans 15:12).
'So that the Gentiles might become an offering acceptable to God, sanctified by the Holy Spirit' (Romans 15:16, NIV).

No wonder St Paul had opponents, people who couldn't believe it, people who looked at 'Gentile sinners' claiming to follow Christ and all they could see were unnatural branches grafted into their vine. It wasn't right. Make them do it properly! But it was happening properly, and wonderfully, and – naturally.

Naturally superior?

It's a difficult word – 'natural'. Yesterday, whilst looking up something for this book, I came across an article that was quite clear gay sex wasn't 'natural'. The way the word was used in that article was loaded with moral meaning. Today, as I showered, I noticed my shower gel claims to consist of 'natural' ingredients. I'm pretty sure a bottle of soap isn't trying to persuade me of its moral superiority – it's a marketing ploy. In the same way, back in my early thirties I was blond for a year – lots of people were at the time. That's my excuse. And I had enough hair for it to matter. Happy memories. Anyway, I recall that a group of us went to a karaoke evening on Aberystwyth pier, and the compere commented as I got up to sing, 'At last, a natural blond.' All my mates laughed. No one thought any character judgements were being made.

When St Paul uses the word 'natural' he too does so without any moral judgement. We read of men and women who 'abandon natural relations' in Romans 1[53] but we need to be biblically literate and not morally prurient when we see that line. The Scripture interprets the Scripture, and St Paul uses the same word for 'natural'[54] in Romans 11 as he does in Romans 1. 'Natural sexual relations' and 'unnatural ones' in Romans 1 take on quite a different tone when placed in the context of the Jew/Gentile discussion of Romans 11. The Gentiles belong to a wild olive tree, and are grafted into the tree of God's people 'against nature', with the Jews being 'natural branches', able to be grafted back in when they respond to Christ.

The imagery is, absolutely, rife with overtones of righteousness and idolatry, of belonging to God or to the gods of the nations, but a cheap superior judgement of others' sexual behaviour as 'not quite the thing' is simply absent.

---

53. Romans 1:26-27 NIV; NRSV has 'giving up natural intercourse'.
54. Romans 11:21, 24: *phusin*.

Cheap moral judgement never has a place at God's table. There's something far more costly at issue. Jesus' death and resurrection deal with the fundamental human failure of all humanity, natural Jew and unnatural Gentiles alike, caused by the fundamental sin of the absence of knowing God in all the nations.

You see, 'no longer Jew or Greek' is not a liberal humanist statement about modern attitudes to racism. It is not St Paul's commitment to the FA's 'Kick It Out' campaign.[55] It is much, much more. It goes much, much deeper.

Hope for all

Biblically, 'no longer Jew or Greek' was entirely about sin. Because of the gift of God, one of these categories (in a traditionalist telling of the Old Testament story) might lay claim to all of God's promises and, because of their sin, the other might never be able to do so, and yet St Paul says –

Through Christ there can be no dividing wall, no barrier separating people into better or worse, no second-class humanity, no moral underclass, no in or out, favoured or disgraced, Jew or Gentile, male or female, slave or free – or any other category we can devise. That's the real telling of the fulfilment of the Old Testament story, the real fulfilling of all God's promises. That's the true wonder of his word.

Modern society wants equality to go at least skin-deep.

Jesus has no interest in us being so superficial. Our problems are not so shallow, and his solutions are far, far more searching.

---

55. www.kickitout.org

You see, I can never accept that the Bible talks about gay and straight simply as a sin issue, with gay people in any way being understood to be 'more sinful' than their straight counterparts just because we are gay. The often deeply harmful results of this unbiblical way of thinking are clearly revealed in the excellent recent autobiographies by Jayne Ozanne[56] and Vicky Beeching,[57] and in the heart-rending *Space at the Table* by Brad and Drew Harper.[58] The UK government is beginning to understand this, putting forward (in the month Vicky and Jayne's books were both published) a 75-point action plan to tackle LGBT inequality,[59] featuring among its aims an end to 'conversion therapy', one of the major weapons of those who confuse gay people being different with gay people being more 'sinful', and a common factor in the life stories told in the books I just mentioned. Steve Chalke, in welcoming this plan to end conversion therapy, adds that for many who suffer such spiritual discrimination, it is not actually the full-blown conversion therapies that are the problem. It is simply the pastor who offers a young person informal prayer to 'help them' which can be devastating. The preaching which casually includes 'same-sex attraction' along with other 'common problems' such as lying, drinking, lust and so forth.[60] The little things that come without thinking when 'Gay' means 'Sin' and when 'Sin' means 'Moral Failing' and when 'Moral Failing' means 'Not Like Me'.

Look: of course 'no longer Jew or Greek' is about sin. Only (and here is St Paul's great double-edged surprise) sin is first

---

56. Jayne Ozanne, *Just Love*, Darton, Longman & Todd, 2018.
57. Vicky Beeching, *Undivided*, William Collins, 2018.
58. Brad and Drew Harper, *Space at the Table*, Zeal Books, 2016.
59. See: https://assets.publishing.service.gov.uk/government/uploads/system/uploads/attachment_data/file/722320/LGBT-Action-Plan-Command-Paper.pdf
60. See: http://openchurch.network/content/5-damaging-practices-churches-inflict-lgbt-people

and foremost about our brokenness from God, our worship of something else in his place, our spiritual state, *not* our moral lives. And also (crucially, amazingly, shockingly, gloriously) both Jew *and* Greek are sinful. So the model of no longer Jew or Gentile tells us that there is absolutely no chance of a barrier, no inkling of a special case here, no glimmer of an option of regarding anyone as better or worse because all have sinned and fallen short of the glory of God, and all are justified freely though his grace. All. For goodness' sake, if Jews and Greeks are equal in God's eyes in his Church, then every saint and every sinner in every category gets the same treatment.

By God's great mercy, people are people.

The point of Galatians 3:28 is not that male/female, slave/free, Jew/Gentile just don't matter any more. It's much, much more than that: there is now in Christ one new, equal humanity. That's a revolution. Paul sees how Jesus deals with us and has no other conclusion. <u>All have sinned. All get the gift.</u>

The remarkable thing is that, in a culture which knows all about giving and receiving gifts, but where there is a very clear understanding that worthy gifts go only to those who are worthy to receive them, this gift, the greatest gift, goes to the unworthy. And the sting in the tail is – that's everyone. That's the offence of Paul's gospel to the Jewish community. We fixate on Romans 1 and find it unpalatable in our day; Paul would be amused. In his day it was Romans 2 that caused the fuss! The Jews got no free pass! More – no pro-Jewish change was required of those coming into the trajectory of hope, the story of redemption that he told about Jesus. That's the reason for the Council of Jerusalem in Acts 15. That's the whole tale of Galatians. There is one, new, equal humanity in Christ. One remarkable gift, given freely, and it is for all – unworthy as we are – and it is for us.

So when we develop some new cultural division, some new cultural barrier that we haven't thought about before, some new way of devising a moral underclass, some new focus for a two-speed humanity with some minority being made second class, Galatians 3:28 is always freshly vital. It doesn't matter that it doesn't mention the case at hand.

We've already dealt with it.

Beginning in Jerusalem . . .

This isn't a moment's aberration, a blip, a sideline in St Paul's main thinking. This is core stuff in his understanding of how the Church is to work. One Lord, one people.

It was like this at the start for him. It was like this at the end.

Let's go to the Council of Jerusalem. In Acts 15 we get the first great conflict between the Jewish and Gentile believers. Paul and Barnabas travel to Jerusalem to meet with the leaders there to argue for the Gentiles that they should not be regarded as second-class Christians. There were some who said that Gentiles needed to be circumcised, needed to take on Moses, needed to adopt full Jewish practice in order to be part of the family of Jesus. Paul said no – and Peter agreed: 'Now therefore why are you putting God to the test by placing on the neck of the disciples a yoke that neither our ancestors nor we have been able to bear? On the contrary, we believe that we will be saved through the grace of the Lord Jesus, just as they will' (Acts 15:10-11).

A yoke no one could bear . . . The weight of prejudice is indeed an old story.

Paul follows up with tales of how God has been working among the Gentiles with great power, and James comes to the judgement – with his words preserved in a letter to be distributed among the small, burgeoning, scattered congregations of non-Jewish believers: 'For it has seemed good to the Holy Spirit and to us to impose on you no further burden than these essentials: that you abstain from what has been sacrificed to idols and from blood and from what is strangled and from fornication. If you keep yourselves from these, you will do well' (Acts 15: 28-29).

From our standpoint, this seems an odd collection of requests. Yes, everyone is a believer by faith in Jesus, hallelujah, and by the way, please do avoid food sacrificed to idols, and would you mind awfully respecting our food laws generally and, oh yes, don't have sex outside marriage.

That's pretty much how these things get heard.

Well, of course, that's not what is being said. Peter is clear – Jew and Gentile both are saved by the generous gift of God, not by morality or lifestyle choices. The generous gift of God is a righteousness that cannot be earned. A right relationship. A life of worship, where we creatures again love our wonderful Creator.

Perhaps a passage like Deuteronomy 12 was in the apostles' minds as they gathered in Jerusalem. In that chapter we are reminded how all the false places of worship, all the tiny shrines and temples to things that are not God are to be broken down, so no sacrifices can be made in those places. No false sacrifices. There are good and proper gifts to be offered to God in the right place – and when that happens, the blood of animals is poured out as an offering, separately. And in God's holy Temple, God's people become more human, not less; they don't forget themselves in the orgies of the pagan places, they find themselves in the worship of the true God of love and service.

The encounter of Paul with the Jerusalem church in Acts 15 entirely fits with his theology in Romans 1.

Because James' call for abstinence from food sacrificed to idols, from blood and from fornication can never be about a narrowly applied morality: it is always about a larger freedom to live in full relationship with God. Brokenness and righteousness. And that is never just a story aimed at gay people, however convenient such a story may be. In fact, it's a downright inconvenient story but a glorious one – idols and blood and fornication were all, always, the symbols of pagan worship; grace and life were the promises of a new worship that made sense. For everyone. James writes – Welcome! Now let go of the old. Fully embrace the new. No idols. Know Jesus.

Welcome, straight people. Let go of the old. Fully embrace the new. Welcome, gay people. Let go of the old. Fully embrace the new. Welcome men, welcome women, welcome slaves, welcome citizens, welcome all.

To twist this as a moral demand is to have a 'Jesus plus something else' gospel. The very thing St Paul opposes at Jerusalem, opposes at Galatia, opposes at Colossae –

Ah yes. Same message in Colossians. We haven't finished yet because St Paul hasn't finished yet. Galatians 3:28 isn't a one-off. Its clarion call for inclusivity and its ringing cry through the ages that God has changed the whole playing field for all of humanity sounds louder and louder.

Here's Colossians 3:11 – 'there is no longer Greek and Jew, circumcised and uncircumcised, barbarian, Scythian, slave and free; but Christ is all and in all!'

Put to death the things of idolatry, says St Paul at the beginning of Colossians 3. He doesn't aim this at gay people, just at – well, people. From immorality – what people do – to evil desires – what they think – St Paul says, break with the old life. He uses language straight out of Romans 12 as he writes: 'you have stripped off the old self with its practices and have clothed yourselves with the new self, which is being renewed in knowledge according to the image of its creator' (Colossians 3:9-10).

And it is in this renewal that there is no longer sinful Greek or self-righteous Jew or any other division we make between us. No circumcised or uncircumcised. No slave or free. We may well add – no straight or gay.

Why may we add this?

Because for St Paul the remaking of humanity in one new body by Christ is a fundamental understanding of what Jesus has done. The depth of just how second-class Gentiles were in the eyes of some within the earliest church cannot be overstated. And St Paul will not have it. Gentile sinners no more. Still Gentiles, but now God's. Not separate. Not broken. Chosen, holy and beloved (Colossians 3:12).

If it is true here, it is always true. St Paul writes a new law for God's people, an unbreakable law of inclusion that welcomes in every person as a sinner loved by God just as every other person is. A frail, fragile human being made in an unspeakably holy image and given the priceless gift of walking hand-in-hand with their Maker and Redeemer and Friend.

I weep when I read St Paul, for here is someone who understands my needs and fights for me. For everyone who was ever made to feel especially sinful. For us all.

And he's still not done.

The Gentiles' charter in Ephesians 2 is something all of us who are not Jews by heritage hold on to as our spiritual right. It has nothing to do with race. It is about sinners excluded by those who see themselves as the only righteous ones – it is about the second class, the more sinful being shown that they are not second class, not more sinful, they are the glorious recipients of grace along with any and everyone else.

It is a wonderful song gifted to us by St Paul that every excluded person everywhere needs to sing out proudly:

> So then, remember that at one time you Gentiles by birth, called 'the uncircumcision' by those who are called 'the circumcision' – a physical circumcision made in the flesh by human hands – remember that you were at that time without Christ, being aliens from the commonwealth of Israel, and strangers to the covenants of promise, having no hope and without God in the world. But now in Christ Jesus you who once were far off have been

brought near by the blood of Christ. For he is our peace; in his flesh he has made both groups into one and has broken down the dividing wall, that is, the hostility between us. He has abolished the law with its commandments and ordinances, so that he might create in himself one new humanity in place of the two, thus making peace, and might reconcile both groups to God in one body through the cross, thus putting to death that hostility through it. So he came and proclaimed peace to you who were far off and peace to those who were near; for through him both of us have access in one Spirit to the Father. So then you are no longer strangers and aliens, but you are citizens with the saints and also members of the household of God, built upon the foundation of the apostles and prophets, with Christ Jesus himself as the cornerstone. (Ephesians 2:11-20)

Christ has broken down every barrier, no matter what others may call us, and even if once we had no hope, we have been brought near to God by Jesus. By Jesus. Not by rules and by the permissions of people. For he is our peace – peace with God, and, gloriously, with each other too. Though the battles still rage, the Prince of Peace will win the day. He is breaking down walls of hostility between us, conquering oceans of misunderstanding, creating a whole new humanity because all of us have access to God through his Spirit. So we're not second class. We're not less. We are citizens, family members, same as, we're part of this story and we're here to stay – built on the same faith of the same apostles and prophets, held up and cherished by the same Jesus.

St Paul hates gays? What utter tosh. His fight for Gentile sinners, which pretty much all of us in the Church today rely on or we wouldn't be here, was nothing less than the fundamental recognition that all people everywhere are fully equal.

No exceptions.

CHAPTER FOUR

FULLY EQUAL

If people are people, if there is no moral underclass and we are all offered the gift of belonging to one, new, equal humanity in Christ then there are consequences that follow.

Let me be clear: I believe that the scriptural witness has no impediment for loving, committed gay relationships. I believe that equal marriage can be encouraged in a Christian setting. But I have every respect for those who disagree – and who, from personal experience, live out the integrity of that choice.

After all, when we started I described Anglicanism as a 'Big House', and went on to see evangelicalism in the same light. These are my home stables within the Christian community, this is where I belong, and it's never been my mission in these pages to convince everyone to agree with me, or to prove that my way of handling the Scriptures is the only way. That's not how we work on a hundred other topics not necessary for salvation, and it's not how we need to work here. It's possible to differ – as long as we are doing so with open Bibles, open hearts, honest faith and genuine desire to be true to Jesus and godly in how we live our lives.

We need to look at some differences and respect them, rather than explain them away or give them a hierarchy of 'correctness' (judged by a multitude of different standards). If we are Christians, following Jesus and living under the authority of his word, respect is the smallest thing we owe one another. It's but a part of the love he requires of us.

Let me say that I have every respect for those who choose the path of singleness and celibacy because (apart from anything else) whatever my beliefs are, that's my life too. One day my life may change. Or it may not. Though at times I have struggled with singleness and celibacy, I knew the moment I wanted to put myself forward for ordained ministry that this was what was expected of me, and I accepted it. So I know that when you have the track record of someone like Vaughan Roberts, whom I have already mentioned, you deserve respect.

Now: I disagree with Vaughan's conclusions that celibacy and singleness are right for every Christian who finds they are attracted to people of the same gender. I believe that same-sex marriage can find a biblical validity. But before I go anywhere near there, I also feel it's right to celebrate the very biblical lifestyle option that traditionalists insist upon.

Celebrating celibacy

Let me be as clear as I can be: celibacy is not a bad option. It can be a terrific option. My only difference with those who propound it as the only option is that they see it as the necessary lifestyle for Christians who are gay, and I do not. I will always commend it as good – within biblical parameters.

Good – yes. Difficult – often. Glorious – sometimes! And by no means the exclusive preserve of gays. But whether you are single, celibate and straight, or single, celibate and gay, I feel like I should apologise. So on behalf of the whole Church of God, here we go – I apologise. I understand what you must go through.

You arrive at a new place. A new church. A new social setting. You're on holiday and meet a group of people. And within minutes you are asked –

'So, do you have a family?'

Of course, if you are young and it's one of those Christian holidays where you're hoping to meet someone, your answer may be very different. But if you have passed the first moments of youth and you are fed up of the way the Church (especially, perhaps, evangelicalism) revolves around couples and families, it can be a most dispiriting moment.

My usual answer is to smile and say, 'No, just me and a springer spaniel.'

Now, I know that as I stand there, glass of wine or cup of coffee in hand, the person I'm talking to is looking at me and thinking, 'But you look quite normal' or (more bluntly) 'But you don't look gay.' A couple of weeks ago, someone actually said that second statement to me out loud. Seriously.

Of course, I don't really mind. I'm old enough and ugly enough to laugh and enjoy such moments. But then – I've been through it enough to find it funny. Mostly. For those who struggle a bit more, may I apologise on behalf of every thoughtless soul out there.

I'm afraid it's just how people think these days. If you are over a certain age and single – there must be a reason. That's what goes through people's minds. I'm a pastor; I've had it explained to me, with people not realising they were saying it about me. Glorious. Of course, a lot of the time in the Church, as in the wider world, being single comes with complications and all sorts of stories – I look at my friends list on Facebook and find that a number of my single Christian friends turn out to have had sexuality struggles of various kinds through the years. But not always. And yet we all get the same response. So I'm sorry.

Why?

Am I apologising that straight single people are (for a moment) being presumed gay? No. Not at all. You should be so lucky. I'm apologising because culturally (once we're past student years) the presence of a single person often seems to bring a certain discomfort into a gathering. People just panic. A single person! Help! I apologise because we are treated as if there's something wrong with us.

Newsflash: single people are normal.

A normal gift

Normal. Not better. Not worse. John Stott is careful to help us hold a scriptural balance. In an interview about singleness, given in 2011, he drew on the experience of his own life but was quick to ensure that those who have suffered from thoughtlessness on either side of the married/single divide don't claim a moral superiority. He said:

> We must never exalt singleness (as some early church fathers did, notably Tertullian) as if it were a higher and holier vocation than marriage. We must reject the ascetic tradition which disparages sex as legalised lust, and marriage as legalised fornication. No, no. Sex is the good gift of a good

Creator, and marriage is his own institution. If marriage is good, singleness is also good.[61]

In the Scriptures being single is always a normal option – but more than that, it is always a gift, and therefore always a blessing for the wider community.

St Paul, in 1 Corinthians 7, in wishing that everyone followed his way of life – his unmarried way of life – is clear that such a personal wish is slightly beside the point because: 'each of you has your own gift[62] from God; one has this gift, another has that' (1 Corinthians 7:7, NIV). Being married is a gift from God, and being single is a gift from God. Leading either life should mean leading a fulfilling life, as God's gift blesses a person and, through that person, a community.

We get an insight into St Paul's understanding of his own gift a little later in the chapter: 'The unmarried man is anxious about the affairs of the Lord, how to please the Lord; but the married man is anxious about the affairs of the world, how to please his wife, and his interests are divided' (1 Corinthians 7: 32-34). For St Paul, the gift of singleness allows him to be single-minded in his ministry and in serving God's people. The level of that gift to the small churches of his day all around the Roman Empire, and to the global Church of God as it has grown ever since, is simply extraordinary.

However, when turned into a general rule, this is at best incomplete and may become problematic. As Loader writes, 'Paul gives no indication of seeing marriage as an advantage in times of hardship or stress or of marrying primarily for love.'[63]

---

61. John Stott, 'John Stott on Singleness', *Christianity Today*, August 2011, Carol Stream, IL 60188, used by permission.
62. Greek: *charisma*.
63. Loader, *Sexuality in the New Testament*, p. 113.

Indeed, St Paul sees marriage as the bringer of hardship: 'those who marry will experience distress in this life, and I would spare you that' (1 Corinthians 7:28).

No doubt marriage can bring distress; no doubt marriage can soothe distress. A gift has all sorts of seasons. So too celibacy.

I have many single friends in ministry. Like many of my married friends, they work ridiculously long hours and give themselves beyond all reasonable expectations. One of the differences for the singles and the marrieds is that St Paul doesn't seem to recognise the hardships that come from imposed and unending professional loneliness. Where there is companionship, there is support along the way. Where there is none, such support may be harder to come by.

The gift has a cost.

This isn't just true of ordained people.

Celibacy, the single life, requires an ability to live alone that some people have and some do not. It's a gift – a divine charism – given to some and not to others. That's St Paul's understanding.

A gift that costs

I read well-meaning calls for the Church to be better at developing 'friendships' for all, so that those who 'have to' live this life find a better community in which to do so. But I've been reading these calls for thirty years and have only occasionally found anything of the reality that might lie behind such ideals.

Community and friendships and understanding are vital for those called to singleness; but even these concepts cannot support those not called to celibacy yet expected to live it. Just as counselling and support and even prayer cannot prop up those not called to marriage. Ed Shaw's chapter on intimacy misses the point for me because good friendships (which he labels 'intimate friendships', wanting to reclaim the word 'intimacy' from an exclusively sexual connotation) are not just for single people, and too many single folk simply don't find themselves with the kind of church around them that can sustain the sorts of groups of friends he describes.[64] Large university churches can sometimes do this, but then as life progresses, large family churches often struggle.

Gifts are gifts. Impositions are impositions. For singleness/ celibacy to be a normal gift, it must be treasured both as normal and as gift.

St Paul gets this. He knows it. 'To the unmarried and the widows I say: It is good for them to stay unmarried, as I do. But if they cannot control themselves, they should marry, for it is better to marry than to burn with passion' (1 Corinthians 7:8-9, NIV).

'Better to marry than to burn' isn't usually how we begin a wedding service! And I'm not sure I've ever heard this used as a text for a wedding sermon, either . . . Please, context is all – St Paul sees both marriage and singleness as divine gift. The point is, if you don't have the gift of singleness, don't fake it. You will end up pointlessly martyring yourself, and no good can come of that.

Those who pretend to be morally 'better' than they are (for whatever reason) live a lie. How much of a lie depends on how big the pretence is. Pretending I can be single when I cannot is

---

64. Shaw, *The Plausibility Problem*, pp.72-80.

a pretty big lie. And that's often where promiscuity and secret sex and a whole slippery slope of sin sets in. St Paul will have nothing to do with it.

This is why I don't go with those traditionalists who insist – if you are gay, you must be single. It ignores St Paul. It ignores the biblical concept of gift. It presumes. It enforces. It de-humanises. It takes away any sense of normality. And it reverses Jesus' principle about people not being made for the Sabbath, but the Sabbath for people.[65] This principle, a radical re-understanding of one of the Ten Commandments, was explained by Jesus as being given to raise people up, not grind us into the dust. How much more then should this gift of celibacy (gift, not law) lift people up and not bind, reduce, make us feel like sinful failures who are unworthy of God and unequal to our fellow Christians? Yet this is (sadly) too often the result of traditionalist teaching when singleness is made law, not gift, and imposed on all gay people.

The Sabbath and the Creation

In a moment I am going to talk about why I support equal marriage, but before I do, let's stick with the idea of Sabbath for a moment longer.

Those who hold that the traditional view of marriage excludes gay people sometimes do so offering both Torah (Old Testament law) and 'Creation' principles as primary reasons for this. Not only does Leviticus speak against homosexual actions, but – so the argument goes – in the beginning God made people male and female, and it is this union and this union alone that he

---

65. Mark 2:27-28.

blesses. It was so in the beginning and God hasn't changed his mind. Apologies if my paraphrase lacks nuance, but I hope this isn't an unfair summary of an argument that is often presented to me.

It's important we debate scriptural principles. It's important we know parts of the Bible that might sometimes seem obscure. It's important that difficult decisions are taken after weighing the whole of the Bible's teaching.

And it's important as well to recall that in Jesus' teaching on the Sabbath we find a very useful reminder on how we evangelicals are to use the Old Testament Scriptures in this debate.

First, the Torah.

Jesus is clear about the place of the Torah, the Law. 'Do not think that I have come to abolish the law or the prophets; I have come not to abolish but to fulfil' (Matthew 5:17). Yet in Mark 2:23-27, as his disciples pick grain on the Sabbath (which the Pharisees hold to be a breaking of the Law), Jesus defends his disciples with two strokes. A reference to King David and his followers comes first[66] – comfortably making himself equal with David, a thing that would not sit well with the Pharisees. And then, even worse, he produces such a deep interpretation of the fourth commandment that the Pharisees are in danger of losing all their power.

Matthew and Luke also have the line, 'the Son of Man is lord even of the sabbath' (Matthew 12:8; Mark 2:28; Luke 6:5). Mark alone adds this crucial explanatory comment: 'The sabbath

---

66. The story Jesus refers to is from 1 Samuel 21:3-6.

was made for people, and not people for the sabbath' (Mark 2:27, New English Translation).

As he discusses the commandment, Jesus does not simply repeat words ('don't work on the Sabbath') or define words ('and by work we mean . . .') as the Pharisees tended to do. He went to the heart of the words. What is the commandment about?

The two versions of the commandment in the Torah give us slightly differing emphases, and perhaps Jesus in Mark has his eye on Deuteronomy here:

> Observe the sabbath day and keep it holy, as the Lord your God commanded you. For six days you shall labour and do all your work. But the seventh day is a sabbath to the Lord your God; you shall not do any work – you, or your son or your daughter, or your male or female slave, or your ox or your donkey, or any of your livestock, or the resident alien in your towns, so that your male and female slave may rest as well as you. Remember that you were a slave in the land of Egypt, and the Lord your God brought you out from there with a mighty hand and an outstretched arm; therefore the Lord your God commanded you to keep the sabbath day. (Deuteronomy 5:12-15)

First we note that the whole social order is included in the benefits of this commandment – the father of the clan, his children, his servants, men and women, those outside the clan visiting, foreigners, and the beasts within their care. The Sabbath is not a restriction but a blessing – for everyone. Children and slaves are granted a full share of humanity as they enjoy the sabbath rest of God's free people.

Back in Exodus, fresh from escaping Pharaoh, Moses reminds the people of the context of God's creation. The Sabbath is about rest. In Deuteronomy, with years between that escape and the imminent entry into the Promised Land, Moses reminds God's people of who they were and who they are to be.

The Sabbath is for everyone – because God's people used to be slaves. They used to live in a land where there was a hierarchy of humanity, with a man who claimed to be like God at the top, powerful men beneath him, angry and brutal men beneath those, and at the bottom – God's people. Slaves. And at the very base of the pile, the women and the children of slaves.

As Moses reiterates this commandment he says: remember that this was not how God ordered life. All are made in his image. Even the foreigner who doesn't know God. So the Sabbath is for all. 'The Sabbath is the great social leveller', as Sean Gladding says.[67] It is given so that we might remember that we are all equally human, and in our freedom might never seek to turn ourselves into Pharaohs (and others into slaves) again.

It is a gift that rings out the love of God and the wonder of humanity. It is not a blind rule or a blanket restriction, and it is certainly not a power tool for the religious authorities to use as punishment over the weak.

This is vital.

This is one of the Ten Commandments, a foundational truth in the story of the people of God, and so Jesus' radical reaching into its heart is all the clearer: simply saying a rule is so does not make it so, even when it is one of the Ten. This is not how God works.

---

67. Sean Gladding, *Ten*, InterVarsity Press, 2014, p. 177.

Again – repeating the words off the page is never enough.

This does not make us evangelical. Words can be present and their meaning absent. Simply quoting stuff can actually make us opponents of God. Jesus opposes those who appear to be promoting the fourth commandment as he reveals them to know only the words, but have no clue at all as to what those words are about and why the commandment is there.

By itself, this should make us very careful about the speed with which we wish to impose other rules from elsewhere in the Torah.

And there's more.

Because the Sabbath rule isn't simply a Law thing. It's a Creation Ordinance.

We have noted that the Exodus telling of the Commandments does not refer to slavery in Egypt. Its rationale for the Sabbath comes in these terms: 'For in six days the Lord made the heavens and the earth, the sea, and all that is in them, but he rested on the seventh day. Therefore the Lord blessed the Sabbath day and made it holy' (Exodus 20:11, NIV).

This is clearly an echo of the opening verses of Genesis 2: 'By the seventh day God had finished the work he had been doing; so on the seventh day he rested from all his work. Then God blessed the seventh day and made it holy, because on it he rested from all the work of creating that he had done' (Genesis 2:2-3, NIV).

The importance of this in our current debate comes as we begin to turn our attention to the question of equal marriage.

Time and again the traditionalist argument uses words from the end of Genesis 2 ('Therefore a man leaves his father and his mother and clings to his wife, and they become one flesh' (Genesis 2:24)) as proof positive that biblical marriage can only be heterosexual. But Jesus has taken words from the beginning of Genesis 2, as used in the context of the fourth commandment, and has made us sit up and understand something really important:

Even fundamental texts must be understood for the true purpose they serve.

The Sabbath is not an imposition of God's order of life upon humanity, but a gift given to bless all humanity. It was made to bless people – all people – not to restrict us. It was made for us, we were not made for it. The commandment exists to help us – even though we trace it back to God's rhythm of creation. Especially as we trace it back to this: for the sun, the moon, the dark, the light, the water, the sky, the animals, the plants, the garden and everything in all creation are God's gifts for his children who, in naming all these things, show that they delight in the gifts given to them.

And if the Sabbath, a part of God's Creation Order and one of the Ten Commandments, becomes a marker of God's generous gifts, a beacon of the equality of all humanity, a sign of freedom from slavery and of the triumph of meaning over literalism, then how much more should all these truths be found in every other part of the story of God and his people?

Jesus knows the detail of the Scriptures, but never gets lost there. Rather, he uses the detail to help us find again the bigger picture we so easily lose.

We only dare to read the Scriptures as if they might exclude people when we already find ourselves believing in a God who chooses to exclude. But Jesus declares himself Lord of the Sabbath so that the powerless are reminded that on every page God makes a different choice.

Good

I said I'd mention why I support equal marriage from the Scriptures – so I will. But – briefly.

Briefly, because actually I think there's something even more important that I want to finish with in a chapter looking at us all being fully equal.

Briefly, because at the end of the day, all I have to offer is my limited, personal reading of the Scriptures. I became a Christian at school when I was twelve. My faith was as much shaped in those early years by my studies of Reformation history as anything else. My sixth-form years were all about the European Church in the sixteenth century, and in the holidays I would read Bainton[68] or Green[69] on Luther, or Parker[70] on Calvin, or anything else that my history teacher threw at me. Sola Scriptura was a truth I learnt in my head and in my heart.[71]

Scripture first

So I struggle to grasp either side of the debate when it indulges in pouncing on detail but leaves the sense and the heart of the Scripture somewhere in the distance. It's easily done – frankly,

---

68. Roland Bainton, *Here I Stand, A Life of Martin Luther*, 1950.
69. Vivian H. H. Green, *Luther and the Reformation*, 1964.
70. T. H. L. Parker, *John Calvin*, 1975.
71. Luther's words at the end of the 1519 Leipzig debates are gloriously problematic, but glorious still: 'A simple layman armed with Scripture is to be believed above a pope or a council without it . . . [N]either the Church nor the pope can establish articles of faith. These must come from Scripture.'

I think we all go there – and let me demonstrate this with a couple of examples from two writers I admire enormously.

N.T. Wright is one of my heroes. It was Tom's lectures on Romans in the autumn of 1990 that first gave me a love for St Paul, a love that has stayed with me and grown year on year ever since. Like so many preachers, when I have no idea what to say on a Sunday (and Sunday is getting really close) it's to Tom's commentaries I turn. His enthusiasm and love of Scripture was a fundamental thing for me in my years at theological college, and remains so today.

But there are times when I find myself pulling back slightly from Tom. He's got a really interesting chapter in *Good Disagreement? Grace and Truth in a Divided Church*, and in it he asks how we tell the difference between things that make a difference and things that don't. How do we know what made a difference for Paul, and what was indifferent for him? Wright's answer – we are the beneficiaries of a lot of very good research in modern times. This makes the difference – and he pulls the best of this together for us. We should trust him.[72]

Hmm. You see, I know I'm going to lay myself open to a charge of being simplistic in a moment, but I struggle with this because help in understanding what is of first-level importance to us, to St Paul (or to any other thing in the Bible) shouldn't be dependent on academics whether of recent generations or from antiquity – an ordinary layperson armed with the Scripture and the Spirit should be able to find the mind of God. I find there's one simple question that gnaws away at me when it comes to all this modern research, and it's this: just which research should

---

72. N.T. Wright, 'Pastoral Theology for Perplexing Topics: Paul and Adiaphora', in *Good Disagreement? Grace and Truth in a Divided Church*, ed. Andrew Atherstone & Andrew Goddard, Lion Hudson, 2015.

we trust? Stuff that agrees with me? Stuff that my Facebook page tells me is good? Anything N. T. Wright publishes? What about the rest?

Tom, in his phenomenal wisdom, goes on in that essay to make an argument for the traditionalist cause. That's not my problem. As I said, both sides indulge in this extra-biblical cherry-picking — so let's be scrupulously fair.

Matthew Vines on the other side of the debate does the same thing. His writing is compelling and innovative and extremely helpful as he brings a sharp mind and an evangelical understanding to bear on these issues from a gay perspective. I'm not sure it qualifies as the kind of 'research of recent generations' that Tom Wright would recommend, but I find Matthew's book, *God and the Gay Christian*, to be a terrific gift to the community.

My hesitation here comes in the chapter 'Will Gay People Inherit the Kingdom of God?' where Matthew Vines discusses St Paul's use of *malakoi* and *arsenokoitai* in 1 Corinthians.[73] By referring to Seneca and Plutarch, he argues that *malakoi* is more properly understood as a word applied to heterosexual men, and by using the Sibylline Oracles and the second century Acts of John he says *arsenokoitai* is better understood as an economic than a sexual term.

Again, I struggle. I mean, on one level what's not to like? If you support a gay-friendly reading, Matthew has just got rid of a problem text!

What's not to like is this: Sola Scriptura. How is an ordinary layperson armed with just the Scripture and the Spirit supposed to understand this stuff?

---

73. Vines, *God and the Gay Christian*, pp.117–31.

I read Matthew and Tom and think the same thing. You need a library, a website, online support and the brain the size of half a planet to start to understand the Bible if they are right about the text. That can't be how God means us to work.

Really clued-up theologians amongst you will be chomping at the bit to tell me that I've got something else wrong though. Lutherans may hold to 'Sola Scriptura', but Anglicans believe in 'Prima Scriptura', which is subtly but importantly different. Not the Scriptures Alone, but the Scriptures First. Not just a layperson and a Bible, and certainly not (on the other hand) a layperson left to the whims of whatever influences and trends of the day may be flying around, with the Bible mixed up as one voice in there somewhere – but the Bible as the foremost tool in our spiritual armoury, shaping and re-shaping every other influence in our lives.

Ian Paul expresses 'Prima Scriptura' with his usual clarity:

> The Church of England does not acknowledge three independent sources of authority in Scripture, Tradition and Reason (as a 'three-legged stool'). Rather, it acknowledges the supreme authority of Scripture which is understood through the hermeneutical (interpretative) lens of tradition (how it was understood in the past) and reason (how we make sense of it in our context).[74]

That's a very fair corrective, but I'm going to stick to my roots when it comes to developing a greater understanding of our important theologies. Biblical understanding should be based

---

74. Ian Paul, 'The Biblical Case for the "Traditional" position'.

on the Bible, and if we struggle to understand the Bible, we need to work harder at it. Other things can help; tradition, reason, all sorts of voices come to our aid. However, if we end up with something we proclaim to be a 'biblical theology' or a 'biblical ethic' and we go on to demand that others live by this stuff – but neither we nor anyone else can actually work it out from the Scriptures alone – well, I think we've crossed a line.

Ed Shaw puts it this way:

> Extra-biblical sources can and do obviously inform our biblical interpretation, but to let them determine it is very dangerous. We become reliant on the latest PhD to hear God correctly, rather than seeking to understand his words in front of us in their original biblical context. You'd have to take a degree in ancient history before you can understand things for yourself.[75]

Well said, Ed.

The Bible reveals the Bible.

I told you I was going to lay myself open to a charge of being simplistic.

Good tree, good fruit

It's not that I'm against academics and academic study – far from it. I first read Luther whilst studying for my 'A' levels,

---

75. Shaw, *The Plausibility Problem*, p. 161.

I read more during my first degree (Modern History) at Oxford and then again for my theology studies in the same university. I spent a year at Cambridge working on my first book. But I am in complete agreement with Ed Shaw here that we don't replace Scripture with the latest PhD or a degree in any academic discipline as we seek to hear God correctly.

Sharp minds are a gift to the Church, just like celibacy or marriage, and just like any gift, as Mike Thompson points out, we get to see if they are for real by the fruit they bear.[76]

As an evangelical, and as a gay man, I am fully aware of the traditions of the Church and the teaching of those who have gone before me. And I am aware of the fruit some of that teaching inadvertently bears. It can grind down. It can make people less. It can reduce. It does not always help people become like Jesus. So I will add my own story to Vicky Beeching's, to Jayne Ozanne's and to Drew Harper's because I too have, honestly, faithfully, to the best of my ability and with the best heart I can, lived under the effects of a traditionalist teaching on sexuality that totally intended to be faithful to the heart of Jesus.

Only, it never came close to offering a John 10:10 way of living. 'Life abundant' was not the result.

So there has to be something better – and I believe there is. And I accept that as I try to offer something else, as I teach something else, I must be judged both by the fruit of my own life and by the value and truth of what I offer from the Scripture. That's what the Scripture demands. Again, Mike Thompson puts that really clearly,[77] but I don't need to read him to know that – it's what the Bible says.

76. M. B. Thompson, 'Division and Discipline in the New Testament Church', in *Good Disagreement?*, ed. Atherstone & Goddard, p. 52.

77. Ibid., pp.48–53.

'Watch out, and beware of the yeast of the Pharisees and Sadducees' (Matthew 16:6).

'There will be false teachers among you. They will secretly introduce destructive heresies [. . .] Many will follow their depraved conduct and will bring the way of truth into disrepute [. . .] They will be paid back with harm for the harm they have done' (2 Peter 2:1, 2, 13, NIV).

The Bible places very strong warnings against teachers of the word who turn out to be false teachers.

Offering something that isn't the traditionalist view is not easy, because I am very aware I might be wrong. The thing is, having lived as long as I have, I am very aware that if we are judged ultimately by the fruit we bear, the traditionalist view is not good enough either. Judging by the fruit it bears, I mean.

When I first started to write this book, I kept thinking of folk younger than me. I kept thinking that maybe I could offer something so that they might have a framework, a biblical alternative that could bring them the sort of hope no one gave me in my youth. The sort of confidence in being who you are and being loved by God and being able to hold your Bible in your hand and your heart and your mind confidently, all at the same time. That made me start this.

Then – just a few days ago I was taking time out of my usual parish life to work on this book. I was sitting outside a coffee shop, having a break, miles away from where I live. And by chance I saw someone I know. An old friend. A clergyman who is coming towards retirement. We fell into conversation, swapping stories and catching up on life. He asked what I was doing in that neck of the woods, and I began to enthuse about this project.

As I did, I could see his reaction, and it took me by surprise. He began to well up. The tears visibly formed in his eyes, and quietly began to roll down his face. He told me that he was gay – though he didn't quite use that word. It's a generational thing. I think I was probably only the third person he's ever told. No, not told: confided in. Again, it's a generational thing. I'm talking about a remarkable, godly, wonderful priest in God's Church. A man who has brought many to faith in Christ. A man who has served faithfully all his life and who – and I had no idea – has suffered uncomplainingly all his life, believing himself to be a deeply sinful and very second-class human being.

Suddenly, I am no longer writing with younger people in mind. I'm writing with all sorts of folk filling my thinking.

It's not good enough to produce an ethic and call it biblical when basically it feels like it says – it's OK to be gay if you bear the pain alone and no one can tell. It's OK to be gay if you face life by yourself. It's OK to be gay if you look like a straight person, speak like a straight person, act like a straight person. It's OK to be gay if you pretend.

What do we imagine the fruit of that will be?

Image

Why do I support equal marriage? (I said I'd get here. Briefly. Here it is.)

Well, I might start like this:

Because the teeny-tiny handful of proof texts used to show that God regards homosexuality as bad do nothing of the sort.

Because there is a trajectory of hope, a story of redemption in the Scriptures for gay people, making us equal in every respect with everyone else.

Because the Scriptures do not make me any more a sinner for being gay than they make anyone else a sinner for being straight; we are all sinners in our brokenness from God, and all redeemed by Jesus equally.

Because celibacy is a gift, and so is marriage, and God gives gifts to the body for its blessing.

Gifts, not impositions.

Because Jesus declared himself Lord of the Sabbath so that the powerless are reminded on every page of Scripture that God makes a choice to reach out and cherish those whom anyone – anyone – dares to think of as being less because they are different. It's a Creation Ordinance. It's a Ten Commandment rule.

And then I might add this:

Following the Church of England's 'Shared Conversations' process on sexuality, in January 2017 the House of Bishops published a report for General Synod as a route map for the way forward for the Church.[78] Its second sentence ran as follows: 'We want to begin by reaffirming the key Christian understanding that all human beings are made in the image of God.' The problem with the report was that it never came back to that theology, and in February 2017 the General Synod took

---

78. GS2055 Marriage and Same Sex Relationships after the Shared Conversations, A Report from the House of Bishops. Available at: http://www.tgdr.co.uk/documents/229P-GS2055.pdf

the unusual step of not taking note of the House of Bishops' report. This meant the report was dead in the water, and forced a second attempt,[79] published in June 2017.

The second paragraph of this new report acknowledged that it was to be about 'us, all of us, as persons whose being is in relationship', and (in slightly fuller language than its predecessor) 'that we are talking about and talking to people, with their immense capacities for joy and for pain, created in the divine image and precious in God's sight in ways we can barely begin to fathom'.

This has been my focus throughout this book.

I have looked at how St Paul in Romans does not make a special case of the sinfulness of gay people, but places idolatry as the fundamental sin of all human beings. The brokenness between us and God. It may play out differently or similarly between gay and straight people, but the moral outworking is secondary; we are in the same predicament and need the same solution. More, when we receive the same gift, we are raised up from obsessions with our own bodies and made part of the One Body that we might live lives of service and love, where all of us find our truest selves, our warmest home. We are all broken, and all redeemable, all unable to point the finger at each other, all grateful for gifts of forgiveness and restoration.

I looked at how the Bible does indeed link being gay with idolatry. It's inescapable. And glorious – because the Bible links being straight and idolatry far more. It links being human with

---

79. GS Misc 1158 Next Steps on Human Sexuality. Available at: https://www.churchofengland. org/sites/default/files/2017-11/gs-misc-1158-next-steps-on-human-sexuality.pdf

idolatry; for the link not to exist would be a mark of difference! Our common need is our common bond, and yet through the Scriptures is a story of hope from death to life, from exclusion to inclusion. This is the tale of Leviticus to Romans, of the glory of Galatians, Ephesians and Colossians, of why St Paul is not against gay people but indeed is our greatest friend. We have to throw away the padlocks on the gates of heaven, be done with fears of any institutional moral underclass, and rejoice that people are people. Not in spite of the Scriptures, but because of them. There is one equal humanity. There were barriers, but Christ has destroyed them – and every time we think up a new one, we go back to Galatians 3:28 (and so much of St Paul's work) to see that everything has already been sorted.

And I looked at Mark and Deuteronomy, with a good dose of Genesis thrown in, to see that the story of the Sabbath shows us that all are made in God's image, and that this gift of the Law, of Torah, is not given to restrict but to bless. This is how Jesus uses the Law. If it's good enough for Jesus, it's good enough for his followers. God does not exclude; any choice we make to do so is based not on his standards but on others that we have picked up along the way, and which we should gladly lay down at the foot of the Cross.

And with all this God-given equality for every single one of us, there's an essential extra step that has to be taken.

The Church of England bishops declare that we are all made in the image of God. They even hint at more with the phrase 'persons whose being is in relationship'.[80] And the essential extra step comes as we ask this further question – so what does it mean for us to be made in the image of God?

---

80. Ibid., Introduction, para. 2.

When I was at theological college, one of the texts we read for our ethics class was David Atkinson's *Pastoral Ethics in Practice*.[81] Nearly thirty years on, Christian ethics have changed in all sorts of ways, but this passage is as strong now as it was then:

> We begin with the foundational truth of our faith: God is a community of love [. . .] The Holy Trinity is a communion of persons in love and communication [. . .]
>
> Just as the Being of God himself is personal communion within the Trinity, so to be in the image of God is to be in personal communion with other persons. Aloneness is not part of God's creation intention. Love in all its aspects [. . .] has its meaning in personal relationships.[82]

When we read in Genesis 1:27 'God created humanity in God's own image, in the divine image God created them, male and female God created them' (Common English Bible), this is not a statement of gender and exclusion, of the natural law of the supremacy of heterosexuality. It's a celebration of relationship and community. More, in the context of the world of patriarchal power that will follow through the text of Genesis, this equality of male and female is a glorious counter-intuitive strike for inclusion and the full humanity of every person. To use one terrific blow for inclusion in one area (oh yes, God does accept women as equal to men) as a strike against inclusion in another

---

81. David Atkinson, *Pastoral Ethics in Practice*, Lion Hudson, 1989.
82. Atkinson ibid., pp61-62, text copyright © 1989 David Atkinson.

(no, LGBTQ people are quite another issue) is not a reasonable position for serious-minded Christians who take the Bible as their rule for life.

What it is, is a reflection of the times we live in. We should celebrate that we have got as far as realising that the first bit of inclusion is true. It's been there as an eternal truth in the Scriptures since the beginning, but we are among the first generations to work it out. As I said earlier, it's within my ministerial life that women have been allowed to be ordained as priests in the Church of England; it's since I started writing this book that they have been allowed to be ordained as bishops.

Sometimes seeing what lies in front of our faces on the pages of the Scriptures is simply a question of choosing to take off the spectacles of ages past.

And with fresh eyes reading the Scriptures that give life, and with a heart full of hope and the Holy Spirit as my comforter, if I as a gay man am as much of a person as any straight person, if I have the gift of salvation and am a member of Christ's body, if the Law exists to bless and to include, and if I am made in the image of a God whose nature is persons in relationship and love –

Then why would a life of singleness and celibacy be an option and a gift to my straight neighbour but a requirement for me? In what way does that suggest we are equally human? Equally free to live in the image of God in which we are both made?

Of course, I support equal marriage. I support equal humanity – because the Bible tells me so.

Choice

Yes, the Bible makes the example of marriage heterosexual, and all the positive biblical role models of sexual relationships are heterosexual. Of course, all of the negative biblical role models of sexual relationships are also heterosexual. References to gay actions get a teeny-tiny look in, and (as we've seen) it's possible that some of those references don't really apply to gay people anyway.

But now we get to make a choice:

In a fallen world, an imperfect world, a world where straight people aren't perfect and where gay people aren't perfect either but where as a Church we want to help people live in God and in love, do we make a text like Mark 10:6-9 an example or a prohibition? Inclusive or exclusive?

> 'But from the beginning of creation, "God made them male and female." "For this reason a man shall leave his father and mother and be joined to his wife, and the two shall become one flesh." So they are no longer two, but one flesh. Therefore what God has joined together, let no one separate.'

Does Jesus say marriage is a man and a wife, and it is, and life and faithfulness and companionship and love are the model and the goal and the joy, and they are – but this is a way of life open to all who bear God's image, and in a world where gay people also love and live and want that faithfulness, companionship and joy, they too may share in it?

Or did Jesus say marriage is a man and a wife, and only a man and a wife, and don't even think of asking about it if you don't comply to this exclusive picture?

Example or prohibition? In early 2017 the House of Bishops' Report 'Marriage and Same Sex Relationships' urges no change on traditional teaching on marriage – quoting this teaching and doing so in a prohibitionary way.[83] But is that the only way to see these words?[84]

We get to ask this question afresh on this issue. To make this choice anew here. Our parents didn't get to do this because the world was different for them. We get to face this one with open Bibles and open eyes and open hearts.

And where once the Church only had one answer, now we have the potential for variety. There is the possibility of difference, and not because the spirit of the age has infected us. Not because some of us are weak on Scripture. Not because some of us care deeply for folk we know and want them to have everything they want. But because on both sides of the debate we love Scripture, we love Jesus and we love people. And because it's only fair to apply the same reading of Scripture we already offer to some folk to everyone.

The inevitable car crash?

Well, that sounds lovely, doesn't it? We all love Jesus and we all want to be fair. Everything is sorted then.

---

83. 'The unity of the Church cannot be detached from our common faith in the gospel of Jesus Christ, and therefore from the teaching through which that gospel is faithfully passed on. In following this approach, the Church of England would be continuing to affirm unequivocally the doctrine of marriage set out in Canon B 30', from Marriage and Same Sex Relationships after the Shared Conversations: A Report from the House of Bishops GS 2055.

84. Even in the Church of England the answer is more complicated: the presenting issue in Mark 10 and Matthew 19 is of course divorce, not homosexuality. The Bishops and General Synod of the CofE allow a much more forgiving line on this topic – giving very pastoral advice in their 2002 paper Marriage in Church After Divorce – suggesting that the same words can be read as example, not prohibition.

Of course, the reality is we may or may not all love Jesus, but we're having a pretty hard time loving each other.

Several UK newspapers posted headlines in early January 2016 about the conference of Anglican archbishops gathered together in Canterbury that week. Words like 'schism', 'fractious', 'fragile', 'inevitable', 'split' and of course 'homosexuality' abounded. That fragile meeting of fractious Primates did not in fact split, though the headlines (and the articles and the comments that came with them) could probably have been written any time since the mid-1980s, and will probably continue to be written for some years to come. The world balefully looks on, and is not convinced by the January truce the archbishops agreed upon under a cold Kent sun. We seem intractably divided; in the eyes of many, the inevitable has simply been deferred.[85]

Anglicanism isn't alone. Also in 2016, the United Methodist conference in Portland, Oregon was described by one commentator as 'confusing even to God'. All votes over Methodist responses to gay issues were finally deferred until a new commission reports back to the conference in an effort to prevent schism.

Well, if arguing for a possibility of difference in attitudes towards human sexuality is actually preparing for the likelihood of schism, wouldn't it be better just to put up with a few battered egos and keep quiet after all? Shouldn't my retiring friend continue to put up with things as he has managed to do all his life, and shouldn't I do the same? Where is the good fruit in teaching something that only brings more splits in the Body of Christ?

---

85. The Church of England stated at its July 2018 General Synod that public debate is indeed being deferred until the Bishops' new teaching document, *Living in Love and Faith: Christian teaching and learning about human identity, sexuality and marriage*, has a core document and resources produced to coincide with Lambeth 2020.

If getting into a car and starting on a journey is inevitably going to result in a crash, shouldn't we all just acknowledge that staying where we are is a better idea? Then there would be no scandal, no fractious primates for the press to report on, no lurid pictures of the freshly bloodied Body of Christ for the paparazzi to snap, God would be less confused and we could all get on with what we are supposed to be doing.

Which is what?

> 'The Spirit of the Lord is upon me, because he has anointed me to bring good news to the poor. He has sent me to proclaim release to the captives and recovery of sight to the blind, to let the oppressed go free, to proclaim the year of the Lord's favour' (Luke 4:18-19).

The problem is that we live in a world where the genie is out of the bottle. Despite the wishes – spoken, unspoken – of some, gay people are not silent. They are increasingly not prepared to pretend to be straight. Young people are baffled by the concept that this should even be considered an option. I was born when homosexuality was still a criminal offence, and grew up in a church and society that was shaped by that worldview. People growing up in Britain today are completely free of this. People born now will find it hard to comprehend it was ever so. And the Church's mission of preaching good news, proclaiming freedom, setting the oppressed free and declaring the Lord's favour is – must be – to one and all.

> 'For God so loved the world that he gave his only Son, so that everyone who believes in him may not perish but may have eternal life' (John 3:16).

Everyone who believes.

We can't, as a Church, say – let's not get into the car, let's not go there.

We have to go there, because it is our mission. And if we go there and have nothing to say to all sorts of people we meet, or our opening gambit is – OK, lovely to see you, we really welcome you, now do pretend to be like us, and then we can talk . . .

What kind of 'everyone' did we think Jesus meant?

So are we then simply left with the car crash option? Traditionalists and revisionists filling their vehicles with as many Bible quotes as possible and heading at each other at full speed to see who survives?

The Fulfilment of the Law

Bishop Michael Curry, preaching at the wedding of Prince Harry and Meghan Markle in May 2018, began by quoting Dr Martin Luther King Jr. He said: 'We must discover the power of love, the redemptive power of love. And when we discover that, we will be able to make of this old world a new world, for love is the only way.'

St Paul expresses the 'redemptive power of love' in this way:

> Owe no one anything, except to love one another; for the one who loves another has fulfilled the law. The commandments, 'You shall not commit adultery; You shall not murder; You shall not steal; You shall not covet'; and any other

> commandment, are summed up in this word, 'Love your neighbour as yourself.' Love does no wrong to a neighbour; therefore, love is the fulfilling of the law. (Romans 13:8-10)

I've already referred to some chapters from the book *Good Disagreement?*[86] and I want to focus for a moment on one of the contributors to that book.

Years ago, just before I started my theological studies, I spent six months travelling around the US. During that time I met all sorts of people. Some have remained lifelong friends.

Amongst them was the then curate at the Episcopalian cathedral in Little Rock, Arkansas. Tory Baucum is a man I admire for all sorts of reasons. I admire him for his faithfulness to God, for his leadership skills, for his speaking style, for his use and understanding of the Scriptures, for the way I always come away from his sermons inspired and closer to Jesus, for his prayerfulness and for his desire to love people and bless the Body of Christ.

These days, Tory and I occupy different places in the sexuality debates. He is rector of one of the ACNA[87] churches. A traditionalist. But he remains for me one of my key friends and influences in life.

There are times when you read something and agree with it so much you want to weep. That's how I feel when I read things by Tory. His chapter in *Good Disagreement?* is glorious.

---

86. *Good Disagreement? Grace and Truth and a Divided Church*, ed. Atherstone & Goddard, Lion Hudson, 2015.
87. ACNA – Anglican Church in North America; as opposed to TEC – The Episcopal Church. In Britain, and the rest of the Anglican Communion, talk of schism is theoretical; in the US it has happened.

Grace before truth

Tory writes: 'In the work of peacemaking, grace and truth are not opposed. Especially if we follow the biblical order: grace before truth (John 1:14).'[88] It is that sense of grace, of gift, that we need when we search for a way forward here. It is simplistic to think that every layperson and an open Bible is the answer – except that every person and a Bible has the Spirit, and with the word and the Spirit we are fully equipped to know and serve God and one another. When we struggle, as here we are struggling, it is not to the wisdom of the world that we turn, but to God. Seeking his gifts. Seeking him. The car crash is not the inevitable outcome.

And if we do not have clear alternatives yet, it is perhaps because we have not trusted long enough in the basic grace of our God.

Tory has the kind of experience that gives him the right to write about these things, and to ask all of us to continue together. His congregation committed themselves to helping homeless people, and learned from them that buildings are not everything. They had congregation members who worked in the Pentagon but on the tenth anniversary of 9/11 worked with the local Muslim community and held events with them. They made friends. When, as evangelical members of the Anglican Church of North America, they lost their church building in a long legal dispute with the Episcopal Diocese of Virginia, the Muslims were the first people to offer Truro Church a new home. But Tory had by then taken time to become friends with the Bishop of Virginia, and though they lost the court case, because

---

88. Tory Baucum, 'Ministry in Samaria: Peacemaking at Truro Church', in *Good Disagreement?*, ed. Atherstone & Goddard, p. 177, text copyright © 2015 Tory Baucum.

of the prayerful friendship established between Tory and Bishop Shannon Johnston, the congregation was invited to stay in its traditional home.

So Tory writes: 'Peacemaking is neither making nice nor even the cohabitation of differences. That is cheap and essentially pagan behaviour (see Matthew 5:46-47). Biblical peacemaking, on the other hand, is giving life, restoring relationship, to our adversary.'[89]

Grace, gift, in our disputes – especially the deeply divisive ones – is always going beyond kind words to friends. It is offering a home to enemies. It is friendship with those who are different. It is seen in costly, redemptive love. There is no truth except by grace, and so love is the fulfilling of the law.

Tory is clear. He makes no compromise in what he believes. And it is possible for us to be different and belong together – this is the point.

Perhaps the key possibility for difference is not just that it can be OK for an evangelical not to hold the 'traditionalist' view on sexuality, but that two people fundamentally disagreeing on this can be firm friends and find in each other something of Jesus that inspires and makes them want to grow more like him.

The world expects the car crash. It even wants it – a good catastrophe is great TV.

A deeper grace

We have to disappoint that expectation in order to give a bigger gift, a deeper grace.

After the January 2016 Anglican Primates Conference, there was a lot of reaction from all sides of the debate. The 'fractious

---

89. Ibid., p. 182.

primates' had not ended their week in disarray, but the final communique ended up causing both joy and dismay in equal measure anyway. The Episcopal Church in America was asked to withdraw from certain functions,[90] leading to accusations of a betrayal of LGBTQI people on one side; and yet TEC were not asked to repent, and all the primates agreed to condemn the criminalising of gay people – leading to accusations of weakness and letting go of biblical standards on the other.

A statement from GAFCON (the conservative Global Anglican Future Conference) included the line that: 'The continuing brokenness of the Communion is not the result simply of failed relationships, but is caused by the persistent rejection of biblical and apostolic faith as set out in Lambeth Resolution 1.10. We are therefore disappointed that the Primates' statement makes no reference to the need for repentance.' This was matched by the Rt Revd Marc Andrus of California, who argued in his blog that Dr Martin Luther King Jr would have seen the results of the gathering as 'antithetical to the way of Christ'. His verdict was that the primates 'made peace among themselves by scapegoating the Episcopal Church, and even more fundamentally by further marginalising lesbian, gay, bisexual, and transgendered people. The political powers who plotted the betrayal and execution of Jesus believed that it was expedient to sacrifice one person for the good of order and "peace".'[91]

---

90. '[F]or a period of three years, the Episcopal Church [will] no longer represent us on ecumenical and interfaith bodies; should not be appointed or elected to an internal standing committee; and that, while participating in the internal bodies of the Anglican Communion, they will not take part in decision-making on any issues pertaining to doctrine or polity', Communique from the Primates of the Anglican Communion, 15 January 2016.

91. Bishop Marc Andrus, http://bishopmarc.typepad.com/blog/2016/01/they-did-not-express-the-mind-of-christ.html, 14 January 2016. Both sides of the reac were reported on by Madeleine Davies in 'Reactions Pour in to the Primat Pronouncements', Church Times, 22 January 2016.

At the time, I posted my support for the work Archbishop Justin had achieved in Canterbury, and received strong criticism for my words from some fellow 'revisionists'. I was told privately and publicly that the archbishops were bigots and oppressors, and being nice about it couldn't hide the desperate truth of their awfulness.

Justin Welby himself published his reflections afterwards: he spoke of the pain of everyone on all sides, and especially of the way the Church was very guilty of mistreating gay people. He spoke of the gift of the Church as family, and how there came a moment in the gathering when there was a commitment to be together because it was clearly right. His words are worth reading in full[92] and end with this thought: 'If Christ's flock can more or less stay together, it's hope for a world that tears itself apart – a sign of what can happen with the love and mercy of God through Jesus Christ.'

In a world where everyone seems to hate everyone else, where political opponents are now enemies, where divisions are bigger than ever before, we in the Church have to hear those words of Archbishop Welby. We are all very different folk, but very much loved by the same Lord. This is the revolution. St Paul's revolution of one new humanity in Christ. Now of all times is the time to live it out.

s back, I realised I was heading toward
ınd emotional collapse. It wasn't the
'ive with a certain amount of strain

org/speaking-and-writing/articles/archbishop-
ʳbury

and stress in our lives, and when it gets too much, we deal with it in different ways. I know one person who – in similar circumstances – gets physically ill. It's not a physical response for me. It's mental and emotional.

Living as a gay man in ordained Anglican ministry, on the evangelical side of things at that, has never been easy. I used to try to hide in plain sight. I tried to live so no one knew. Looking back, I think I lived, as a result of doing this, with fairly unbearable stress levels most of the time. And when other work/life/anything-else stresses added on top – it got too much.

So that summer found me realising I was heading toward breaking point, and I had no way out. I tried to get life organised. I made sure my church was running pretty efficiently. Autumn happened, and we began to head toward Christmas. There was a specific moment in November when my reality took a side-step left, and then I did my best to live in the strange new world where I found myself.

Even so, it was another month and a half before I completely stopped and asked for help.

And when I stopped, and when I asked for help, I went through all sorts of emotions and responses and thoughts and feelings. I was angry with people in the Church, and grateful to people in the Church. It was people in the Church whom I was hiding from, and that hiding had caused the stress to get me to breaking point. But it was the kindness of people in the Church – both those who (it turns out) were pro-gay and those who would hold a standard traditionalist viewpoint who helped me through those days. Friends.

I had medical help. I had spiritual help. I was exhausted, and most of all I needed time. A lot of it.

And God loved me. And I realised that I was OK. And I was OK. A good catastrophe may be great TV but there is a bigger gift, and I received that bigger gift of love from all sorts of folk in the Church. People who knew and understood; people who knew and did not understand; people who simply by the time they took and the care they gave demonstrated that it didn't matter if I was gay, straight or Australian. They just loved me.

About three and a half years after the world took that side-step to the left, I was in church on Easter Sunday, and I realised with total joy that I was well again. Raised up.

Hallelujah.

Let me be clear: I tell you this not so that you feel for me, and in feeling for me – and others like me – you alter your opinions and give me more time, and perhaps reconsider things I've said in a new light. I tell you this because it is my story, or a bit of it anyway –

And it matters not one jot.

The world we live in encourages us all to adopt a victim mentality, where we all revel in the injustices done to us and fight the endless fight so that those who have done us wrong will (one day) end up paying for their misdeeds.

This is not the Christian faith. This is not the Church of God.

The Bible tells us there was one Victim and now by giving our lives to him, the rest of us get to be more than conquerors.

The possibility of difference is not just about agreeing to disagree on another theological issue, but about 'hope for a world that tears itself apart – a sign of what can happen with the love and mercy of God through Jesus Christ'.[93] It's about grace before truth, leading to 'Giving life to those with whom we are estranged, resulting in friendship which impacts a wider circle of relationships. This is the goal of peacemaking: restored communion.'[94] It's about the people I love who agree with every word in this book and the people I love who don't, but we all belong to one another because we all belong to Jesus and his body, the Church.

It's about us taking seriously Bishop Curry's words in Windsor on that sunny May afternoon: 'Love is not selfish and self-centred. Love can be sacrificial, and in so doing, becomes redemptive. And that way of unselfish, sacrificial, redemptive love changes lives, and it can change this world'.[95]

It's about us choosing to be the Church. For real.

It's about you. And me. And our choice to 'Let no debt remain outstanding, except the continuing debt to love one another' (Romans 13:8, NIV). Not just with our friends, but with the folk we find difficult, objectionable and just plain wrong.

When we all realise that, understand that, live that – then we will have truly embraced the rather glorious possibilities of difference, and will indeed have become the fully equal children of God.

---

93. Ibid.
94. Baucum, 'Ministry in Samaria', p. 188, text copyright © 2015 Tory Baucum.
95. Presiding Bishop Michael Curry, Address at the Wedding of the Duke and Duchess of Sussex, 19 May 2018.

CHAPTER FIVE

REFLECTION

The heat of the morning had all gone. A soft, insistent rain was falling, leeching all colour from the day. It was wet and dull and turning cold.

It was as if the disciples' feelings had infected the weather.

Matthias and Cleopas were as torn as everyone else in the room, but could bear the arguments no longer. One thing they agreed on: they were leaving.

It wasn't just the grief. The loss. The not understanding for a moment what had happened to them. To Jesus. Give them time and they'd get there, eventually. But that morning, some of the women had run into their midst with wild joy and crazy stories, and everyone had wanted to reach out for some new, faint whiff of hope.

Well. Grasping at straws was the final straw. Wild and crazy, or hope returning? Take your pick. Draw your line. Let your grief do the talking and suddenly the room where they gathered was ablaze with recriminations and anger and factions and everything that Matthias and Cleopas wanted to run away from.

Matthias wanted to hope the women had seen something; Cleopas knew better. The two men had been friends for years, but this moment seemed to hold all that time as dust. Like the colours of the day, all that held them together was fading, and as they left the room, the house, the street, the city, there was a sudden sense between them that they should keep their argument going somehow, because soon –

Soon, they'd be leaving each other behind too. For good.

It was the end of a very long day.

So they spoke. Words. Endless, pointless, words. They walked the familiar road out of the city, and re-trod the same old ground of disagreement that they'd gone over all day. Their eyes and hearts cast down, they knew where they were going.

Which is why they didn't notice for some time that they weren't alone.

One was heading south, one north, but they chose to leave by the same west gate so that the final moment of parting was delayed. It was a marginally longer journey for each this way. It made little difference. It felt slightly better that they weren't rushing away from each other. The steep road down from the city grew narrow in places, but even now in the late afternoon there was still traffic going both ways. The two friends found themselves one moment side-by-side, the next walking single file. Neither, afterwards, could put his finger on the exact moment when in that long descent from Jerusalem the two of them had become the three of them. They just realised that the side-by-side was broader. And their conversation slowed with the realising.

The realising made the companions break the unintended harshness of their voices for a moment, both silently wishing the intruder might pass on by. They slowed their pace, allowing whoever this man was to move ahead. But he didn't. He slowed with them.

The rain was slightly heavier now, seeping into their cloaks, and the intruder pulled his garment over his head as he turned to them and asked, 'Sounds serious. What's getting you so wound up?'

For a moment both friends stood completely still, their silence tinged with embarrassment. Though they were walking away from one another, this was a private, shared moment; they didn't want an audience. A week ago they might have been putting their arms around this intruder, ushering him back into the city, encouraging him to come and see all that was going on. Now they were jealously protecting the few moments of friendship left to them, fighting for the edges of dreams spoiled by stupid women and fractious men.

'Have you really been here in Jerusalem and not seen the things that have been happening?' Cleopas eventually replied.

'What things?' came back the answer.

His eyes looked at them intently from under his hooded cloak. He made no move to withdraw. Matthias looked at Cleopas, and Cleopas shrugged. What did it matter?

So they told him as they walked on to where the path would divide. They told him. Everything.

'What things? We're talking about Jesus of Nazareth,' said Cleopas. 'He was a prophet of God, powerful in word and deed.'

'Nazareth? Don't limit it to Nazareth,' replied Matthias. 'And don't reduce him to a prophet. He was much, much more. Everyone knew it. Everyone saw it. He was God's Messiah.'

'Everyone saw it. Sure. Except that our Chief Priests handed over God's Messiah and they crucified him. Everyone saw that.'

Both men were silent.

'Everyone did see that.' Matthias paused, a sob of grief catching him; Cleopas put his arm around his friend as he spoke. 'Only we'd hoped for so much more. I thought he was the one. I really did. I thought he'd change the world.'

'Well, that's hope for you,' said Cleopas. 'Just days ago, everything we touched turned to gold; today we're walking on quicksand.'

Matthias pulled away from Cleopas' arm.

'And that's where you are wrong!'

'Here we go again.'

The three men walked on. Cleopas, his friend Matthias, their new companion. For a moment, there was a sullen silence in the group. The rain hid their tears from each other. Now Matthias pulled his cloak over his head, feeling the first hint of the evening wind rising as the afternoon light began to fade.

Then he carried on the tale, speaking to their new companion, ignoring Cleopas.

'So he died. Three days ago. So we were in shock. So I guess we hadn't even begun to deal with it. Then early this morning some of the women burst into the house where we gather, laughing and crying and making no sense at all.'

'You can say that again,' muttered Cleopas.

Matthias continued to ignore him. 'They'd been to the tomb where Jesus had been laid, to put spices on the body, pay respects, you know – but there's no body. Nothing. It's just an empty cave when they get there. Then suddenly they see angels and light and there's a voice telling them Jesus is alive – so they come running to find us!'

Their new friend made no response before Cleopas interrupted: 'And we all wanted it to be true. Really. All of us. Of course we did. So we sent some of the men back to the garden to see for themselves. And sure enough – empty tomb, no corpse. But no angels either. No voice. No Jesus. No life. Nothing. Face it, Matthias, I don't know what we thought was going to happen, but now we're all going home and it's raining. So that's it. That's all there is.'

For a moment it seemed as though Matthias and Cleopas were not only about ready to resume their argument, but might actually come to blows, when their new companion suddenly put himself in the middle of them: he placed an arm on each of them, and surprised them both with the strength of his reaction.

'Have you two lost it completely? Call yourself Jews – have you never actually read the prophets? Or tried believing what they wrote? Do you not know that of course the Messiah suffers first and then triumphs in glory?'

Matthias and Cleopas stared dumbstruck in shock. They didn't expect this.

'Tell me, where are you going?' asked their walking friend.

'Emmaus,' replied Matthias.

'Bethlehem,' said Cleopas.

Their new friend looked at them from under his cloak in the rain and the failing light.

'My brothers,' he said, 'Forgive me, but please let's walk on together. You can't take different paths like this. Surely you've had enough loss this week without losing each other too?'

'Well, I don't want to go to Emmaus,' replied Cleopas, crossly. 'I want to go to my own home and sleep in my own bed.'

'There's no way I'm going to Bethlehem. The whole place is like a cowshed,' fired back Matthias.

'Well, we can just stand here then,' said their companion, 'or perhaps if you two can't decide, then I get to choose. Bethlehem I know from way back, but Emmaus is new to me. I'm in the mood for new things today.' He turned to Cleopas and smiled. 'Go on, humour me, please.'

And Cleopas, despite himself, nodded.

'Emmaus, good; then we have plenty of time.'

With that, they set off together again.

And beginning with Moses and all the prophets, their new friend told them everything the Scriptures had to say about the Messiah. As he spoke, now for a moment Matthias felt himself justified, next Cleopas felt vindicated, and then increasingly both found themselves forgetting themselves completely as their argument (whatever it actually was) faded. In its place was Jesus. They listened as their companion described Jesus so clearly. They glimpsed again everything they had ever hoped for, and they found in their hearts a burning, yearning sense of their deepest, truest longings. For all the bitterness of their disagreement, they both knew that here was where they really belonged – with this perspective that helped them grasp a better picture, a bigger picture, a clearer picture of Jesus.

It felt again for a moment as they approached Emmaus like it used to feel. Before. And that feeling began to soothe the deep grieving within their souls.

Matthias' house was on the very edge of the village, and he and Cleopas slowed as they reached it. Their companion, however, made as if to continue.

'Stay –,' Matthias called after him. 'Please stay.'

He turned back, wiping the rain from his face, and looked at the two friends. Evening was drawing in quickly now, and he had every intention of stopping. He had almost done his work with them. They had almost understood.

'Yes,' added Cleopas, 'it's late, please have some supper with us.'

He smiled.

In the house, Jesus sat at the small wooden table. He watched Cleopas and Matthias as they prepared the food together. The fire of their argument had gone. They were tired and liable still to strike the odd spark from each other; grief still held them in its tight lock, but the earlier, harsher bitterness of their anger had run its course.

He watched and saw the natural humour of the two friends, the ease of men who have known each other well for many years. He saw peace restoring her place over them.

When he met them outside Jerusalem, they had decided to walk apart. They had given up. He had given them a little more time together, time they had otherwise decided not to have. In his company, before, these dear people had become family, his family. Today he'd reminded them of that.

And he'd taken their eyes off the disaster of his own death which had ripped them apart. He'd stopped them retreading the last seventy-two hours of pain, pain which had removed the previous three years of joy. In talking through all the Scriptures he had put back in their hearts the perspective of all those years. He had reminded them too of the promises of all sorts of times to come.

Grace and truth. Gifts of love. Time and friendship. Simple things to conquer barriers of fear.

Now it was time to finish this. To finish re-envisioning them. To open their eyes fully so that they might never again part and ever again be one in him. Family. United. With a purpose and a message that would change them and everyone they met.

'Are we about ready to eat?' he asked.

'Of course,' replied Matthias. 'And as our guest, would you pray the blessing?'

Jesus paused.

He reached out for the bread, took it in his hands and broke it as he began to pray: 'Blessed are you, Lord God of the Universe . . .'

And as he prayed, he allowed his sleeve to slip a fraction up his arm.

And Matthias saw.

Catching his breath, Matthias reached out his hand, turned slightly and tapped Cleopas' arm. Cleopas frowned, then when he felt the tapping again, opened one eye and looked where Matthias pointed.

He too saw.

They both saw the wrists. The marks. The hands. The bread, broken.

For a split second they turned to one another in shock, then they turned back –

And Jesus was gone.

For a moment, silence. Then both men laughed. They stood, they cried, they hugged.

'Did you see – '

'It was!'

'I knew it – '

'My heart on the road . . .'

'Like fire!'

'Really! Me too!'

A pause.

'We have to go back.'

'And tell the others.'

'It's too late . . .'

'Do you really care?'

'No!'

They ran into the night air. The rain had stopped, the clouds cleared and a cold spring moon hung over the valley, lighting the road all the way back to Jerusalem. Matthias and Cleopas ran most of the seven miles, often singing, mostly out of breath, stopping every now and then simply to look at each other in wonder.

When they got back to the city, they rushed up to the house where most of the disciples were still gathered together and banged at the door.

They were greeted with embraces but for a moment weren't even allowed to speak as everyone in the place spilled out the news that Peter himself had seen Jesus. The women were right!

And then Cleopas and Matthias got to tell their tale, start to finish, though to be fair hardly anyone heard a word they said.

For all the gathered disciples in Jerusalem could see were two men who had left them that afternoon at the end of their friendship, shouting and arguing with each other, ready to leave the city and the fellowship and each other for good.

And now?

And now, as they spoke together of all that Jesus had said and done, they were hardly the same people at all.

ACKNOWLEDGEMENTS

On the day I finished the first complete draft of this text, someone crashed into my car.

Inevitable?

Many thanks to all who helped me deal with that, and for my wonderful hosts that week, Chris and Ruth Holmwood, for giving me a place away from home to write.

Thanks to all who let me bounce ideas around, and who encouraged me to think and speak and work my way through so much. To John and Clare Hayns, who are dear to me beyond words. To Tory Baucum and J. D. Walt, whose care and friendship over many years has shaped my heart and, though we differ on many things, we belong to the family of God together.

To congregations in Pontypridd, Calverley and Oxfordshire who have (often unbeknown to them) found themselves on the receiving end of my theologising on this topic. And who have had more St Paul from me than anyone deserves.

I have been fortunate to be encouraged by a series of very different Anglican bishops – Barry, Nick, John, Colin, Steven. Thank you for wisdom, kindness, time and (at times) showing more faith in me than I had in myself.

And to those few folk who read the long essay I sent to the Pilling Commission and replied with surprisingly positive words, thank you. If you hadn't done that, I might never have done this.

Thanks too to those who kept supplying questions and comments and who pushed me further and further. I should mention especially Tom Fuerst, whose creative energy I love; and Richard Herkes, whose eye for detail and whose belief in this project were remarkable gifts to me.

Thanks to everyone at Kevin Mayhew for taking a risk on me – especially Dave Gatward for his overwhelming support, editor Virginia Rounding, proofreader Linda Ottewell and cover designer Rob Mortonson. And to Jayne Ozanne, whose friendship and belief in this project helped it see the light of day.

There are too many others I need to thank – but I'll settle for Charlie, Matt and Harry, the best listeners in the world, and Gill, the only person I know who is more like a dog with a bone than I am when she's sure she's right.